NEVERMIND

NIRVANA

CLASSIC **ROCK** ALBUMS

Series Editor: Clinton Heylin

NEVERMIND

NIRVANA

Jim Berkenstadt and Charles R. Cross

SCHIRMER BOOKS
New York

Schirmer Books
1633 Broadway
New York, NY 10019

Library of Congress Catalog Card Number: 97-51361

Printed in the United States of America

Printing Number
10 9 8 7 6 5 4 3 2 1

Library of Congress Cataloging-in-Publication Data

Berkenstadt, Jim.
   Nevermind : Nirvana / Jim Berkenstadt and Charles R. Cross.
      p. cm. — (Classic rock albums)
   Includes index.
   Discography: p.
   ISBN 0-02-864775-0 (alk. paper)
      1. Nirvana (Musical group) 2. Grunge music—History and criticism. 3. Rock musicians—United States—Biography. I. Cross, Charles R. II. Title. III. Series.
ML421.N57B4 1998
782.42166'092'2—dc21   97-51361
                                                                                   CIP
                                                                                   MN

As this page cannot legibly accommodate all of the permissions and credits, they appear on page 159.

This paper meets the requirements of ANSI/NISO Z.39.48-1992 (Permanence of Paper).

CONTENTS

ACKNOWLEDGMENTS

The authors would like to thank all those who helped us with the extensive research and numerous interviews required to write this book. Particularly generous with their time and help were Chad Channing, Jack Endino, Krist Novoselic, John Silva, Butch Vig, Andy Wallace, and Howie Weinberg. Special thanks to: Loren Albert; Yeda Baker; Holly; Rebecca and Bradley Berkenstadt; Lois and Edward Berkenstadt; Gene and Laurie Berkenstadt; Edon Berkenstadt; The Big O; Janet Billig; Tom Blain; Jonas Blank; Kelsy Boyd; Jamie Brown; Lenny Burnett; Kelly Canary; Rosemary Carroll; Richard Carlin; Leo Cailleteau; Joy and Jack Charney; Marco Collins; Ernie Conner; Helen and Garvin Cremer; Scott Cremer; David Day; Carla and David DeSantis; Helen English, Esq.; Joe Ehrbar; Lisa Fancher; Scott and Lynne Faulkner; Jeff Fenster; Erik Flannigan; Deborah Frost; Gillian Gaar; Ross Garfield; Lisa Gladfelter-Bell; Clinton Heylin; Steve and Erica Hill; Bill Holdship; Daniel House; Mark Kates; Bonnie Laviron; Debbie Letterman; Darcy Little; Courtney Love; Patrick MacDonald; Leanne Martin; Guy Kenneth McArthur; Jerry McCulley; Carl Miller; Mike Musburger; Shivaun O'Brien; Jacque Oldenburg; Jay Olsen; Doug Olson; Charles Peterson; Christopher Phillips; Michelle Puddester; Bill Reid; *The Rocket;* Jeff Ross; Pauli Ryan; Rex Rystedt; Smart Studios; James Smith; Mark Smith; Sound City Studios; Damon Stewart; Denise Sullivan; Susie Tennant; Kim Thayil; John Troutman; Jaan Uhelszki; Scott Vanderpool; Chris and Renee Vig; Patty Vig; Tess Welch, Esq.; Daryl Westmoreland; Alice Wheeler; Ellen Whitman; Mark Zappasodi; Bob Zimmerman; Mike Zirkel; and anyone whose name we forgot or who helped out at the last minute.

NEVERMIND

It was one minute before seven on the evening of September 16, 1991, and the world of rock 'n' roll was about to change forever. The place was Seattle, Washington. The setting was a small record store in the University District named Beehive. (For years it had been called Peaches, but a recent lawsuit from a record chain in the South had forced a name change. Locals still called it Peaches). The band was a three-piece, and the lead singer had on a gray flannel shirt.

In an early draft of his song "Smells Like Teen Spirit," Kurt Cobain had posed the question, "Who will be the king and the queen of the outcasted teens?", and though he never sang the song with those lyrics, one can only wonder if they ran through his head that early autumn day at Beehive. The answer—being shouted back at the three-piece band by their screaming fans—was loud and clear. It was the name of the band; it was *"Nirvana!"*

What had been planned as a low-key meet-and-greet at one of Seattle's smaller record stores had turned into a crowd-control nightmare. An "in-store" is traditionally a small party put on by a record label to celebrate the release of a new album, and, in theory, it's designed to boost sales by introducing the band to influential record-store buyers. In practice, store promotions are rarely more than opportunities for labels to butter up the bands on their roster, where the group's friends have a chance to sample a free buffet of cheese and crackers paid for by the label. Even in the burgeoning Seattle scene of 1991, it was rare for any in-store to draw more than 100 fans. When the Red Hot Chili Peppers, at the time an up-and-coming national band with a huge following in the Northwest, did

Nirvana—Kurt Cobain, Dave Grohl, and Krist Novoselic—not long after the completion of the *Nevermind* album.
(PHOTOGRAPH BY YOURI LENQUETTE/RETNA)

1

Live at Beehive. September, '91

Kurt-

Your music is there for me when I feel alone. I'm sorry I couldn't be there for you when you were alone. Rest in peace.

Love,
A fan

Kurt Cobain during Nirvana's
Nevermind **in-store at**
Seattle's Beehive Records,
September 1991.
(PHOTOGRAPHER
UNKNOWN.)

an in-store at Beehive, they drew 150 fans. And though the warning signs in the case of Nirvana had been visible for some time—within the underground post-punk world people had been talking about their upcoming major-label debut for months—no one could have predicted what happened on that September day and what would happen in the next six months.

"Kids started showing up at 2 P.M. for a 7 P.M. scheduled appearance," recalls Jamie Brown, promotions manager for Beehive and organizer of the in-store. "We thought there would be a big crowd, but we had no idea they'd be there all day. By 4 P.M. it was jam-packed with about three hundred kids and you couldn't get in the store. The kids just sat on the floor."

By 4:30 P.M., when the band arrived, the three members of Nirvana—Kurt Cobain, Krist Novoselic,* and Dave Grohl—found a record store so crowded that no more people were being allowed in. There was also a crowd of two hundred people milling around *outside* the store in the small parking lot. The trio immediately retreated across the street to the Blue Moon Tavern to escape. Even that did not provide much privacy, as dozens of kids followed the group to the Blue Moon and stared at them through the windows (Washington's liquor laws allowing only those twenty-one and over to enter taverns).

One wonders if, sitting there in the Blue Moon that day—a tavern famous as one of the birthplaces of Seattle's first countercultural revolution during the '60s, and a place where Jack Kerouac once drank— the members of Nirvana had any idea what was about to happen to them. In the five years that the group had been together (that's how long Kurt

*Novoselic changed the spelling of his first name from "Chris" to "Krist" in 1992.

2

Cobain had been jamming with Krist Novoselic; Dave Grohl was already the band's fifth drummer), Nirvana had witnessed a steady growth in popularity. They'd gone from playing for twenty uninterested alcoholics at Seattle's Central Tavern to headlining gigs drawing as many as a thousand people. Their first record, *Bleach,* had received positive reviews, and if it hadn't sold tremendously to that point—the Sub Pop label estimates that they had sold forty thousand copies of *Bleach* by September 1991—it had sold enough to create a buzz that fueled a major-label bidding war for their follow-up album. That album, *Nevermind,* was due to be released officially in eight days, but stores in the Northwest like Beehive would begin selling copies later that evening, selling them almost as fast as they could cut open the boxes. Drinking Rainier beer that day in the Blue Moon, the band could be confident that their new record would be a success by the standards of alternative rock at the time.

The reason the band drew such a large crowd to Beehive that day was because they'd played so many shows in the Northwest that they had a huge following already; their fans were willing to stand for hours and wait in a cramped record store. Yet what was decidedly different about this new album, and about the show that Nirvana put on that day at Beehive, was that it didn't just impress people: it left many listeners stunned. Some, including Jamie Brown, were shocked that Nirvana had agreed to turn what had been advertised as a meet-and-greet into an impromptu performance. But if most in the crowd were surprised to see the band actually playing inside this small record store, they were even more moved by the performance the band put on at Beehive. "We just jammed," recalls Krist Novoselic, Nirvana's bass player, of the Beehive show. "We were totally on."

His sentiments are echoed by those who were in the crowd that day. "It was stunning and it was beautiful," says John Troutman, an early fan who worked for a different record company at the time but still dubbed dozens of copies of *Nevermind* for friends. "It was simply amazing," says Susie Tennant, the local rep for Nirvana's label, DGC. "I just didn't know what to think," remembers Erik Flannigan, a Seattle journalist who witnessed the event. Flannigan says the performance, like the album itself, left many in the audience in awe: "I don't know that anyone was prepared for it." While most good rock records leave listeners tapping their feet, *Nevermind* left people dazed and confused.

During the show at Beehive you could see that amazement in the stunned expressions on people's faces; a crude bootleg video of the event illustrates that the few fans who weren't moshing were simply staring in wonder. Two teenagers stood in the front row, literally six feet away from Kurt Cobain, and their jaws hung three to four inches below their noses, as if they had no control over their bodies. That "dropped jaw" reaction was something that would be repeated all over the world in the next few months.

If the band had any idea whatsoever of their power, it wasn't apparent to anyone who talked to them during that month of September 1991, and it certainly didn't show at Beehive. When the band finally left the Blue Moon Tavern—fortified with beer to better handle their first promotional efforts at pushing their new major-label album—they snuck in the back way at Beehive and hung out in the basement lunchroom of the small record store. "I remember sneaking down to the lunch room just to catch a glimpse of them," recalls Mike Musburger, one of the many Beehive employees who was also a local musician (at the time, his band, the Posies, were considered more successful than Nirvana). "Kurt was just kneeling there in the middle of the room, writing the set list out on a sheet of paper. There was no hype and they didn't act like big shots or anything. But there still was this air about him. Of course, he didn't create that air—it came more from all the other employees who were watching him."

Though most of the store's workers just stood around and stared at Cobain, Brown says that wasn't because the singer was unfriendly. "At the time, the Seattle scene was such a close-knit thing, even for people who weren't necessarily playing music, that it wasn't like *anybody* was unapproachable," he says. "Everybody prided themselves on being down to earth and not acting like rock stars. Yet the buzz that Kurt created with Nirvana made him that way whether he liked it or not. People were in awe of him and what he was doing." Not that Cobain would have noticed. "None of the band seemed particularly nervous," remembers Susie Tennant, who ushered them around that day. "It wasn't like Kurt to get a big head. But when we all went upstairs, it was a madhouse. I'm not sure anyone was ready for that."

"That" was a record store overflowing with fans, at this point perched any- and everywhere. There were so many people outside the store who couldn't get in that employees eventually shooed them away from the glass, fearing that it might break from all the leaning and pressing against it. "Inside the store there were people standing on top of the racks of albums," recalls David Day, one of Beehive's employees. "There were kids everywhere." The store was so jammed that Day and Brown remember urging the owner of Beehive to go home, fearing that he would cancel the show if he realized how much damage was being done.

Within the crowd of three hundred that Brown estimates were packed into the store was a virtual "who's who" of the Seattle music scene. Members of Tad, the Screaming Trees, the Posies, the Fastbacks, Love Battery, and several other Seattle bands were there to root on Nirvana. Even the members of Soundgarden stopped by—and at that point they were arguably the biggest band in town, themselves preparing for their own major-label album, *Badmotorfinger*. But like many local industry types, the Soundgarden members left because it was simply too crowded. "We were coming from rehearsal, and we were in the area, so we thought, 'Let's go see those guys,'" remembers Kim Thayil, guitarist for Soundgarden. "But it was so damn crowded that we decided to go do something else. It was pretty unbelievable that it was that crowded."

The show began with Kurt softly muttering "Thanks for coming," though that introduction was followed by two minutes of tuning. A few people clapped; this was an audience made up of fans of *Bleach*. There was no stage normally set up in Beehive, so the group played on the same level with most of the audience, which meant that the vast majority of the crowd couldn't see; most people in the back couldn't hear, either, because a wall of people is an effective muffling device. "The crowd actually was on a slightly higher platform than the band," remembers Flannigan. "And since Kurt was short to begin with, it made it impossible to see him, and if you were at the back, you couldn't hear much, except the bass and drums, because the crowd insulated much of the sound." But none of this stopped the audience from getting excited. In the front row, the audience was so close to the band that Krist Novoselic had to make sure he didn't bean anyone with his bass as he swung it around.

Nirvana began with "Drain You," and from that moment on the crowd slam-danced their way around Beehive, forgetting that this was a record store filled with compact discs, albums, and videos, forgetting that there were light fixtures and display racks everywhere, forgetting that the crude PA system wasn't set up to re-create a true concert experience. But even if the conditions were less than optimal, the band made up for it with their performance, playing like they were in an arena rather than a record store. This was no unplugged Nirvana: Kurt began the show by turning up his amplifier to the highest setting, and several times during the performance he tried turning it up higher. He broke a string halfway through "Drain You," though that didn't diminish his intensity, as he played with a ferocity that seemed at times almost demonic.

"The performance was amazing," recalls Kelly Canary, a Beehive employee at the time and also a member of the legendary Northwest punk band Dickless. "In a record store with neon lights on, and in an overall bad place to play, they played great. I'd seen them many times before, but I don't know if they were ever better."

Most of the songs the band played that day were from the yet-to-be released *Nevermind*. Though Nirvana had done a short European tour earlier that summer, much of the material was still new to them. Since recording the album in the spring, they had not played live in Seattle, which was ostensibly their hometown, though in September 1991 none of them lived there. Yet even though *Nevermind* hadn't officially been released, every song they played that day was met with a cheer of recognition from the audience, and many in the crowd sang along. And when the group broke into the first bars of "Smells Like Teen Spirit," it was almost like explosives going off in the room.

"What I remember being most struck by," says Flannigan, "was the fact that the album wasn't even out yet, but that every kid in that store knew the lyrics and sang along to 'Smells Like Teen Spirit.' I'd heard an advance copy of the album and I knew it relatively well, but I just couldn't believe that all these kids already knew the song way before the album had even come out. And I knew at that point that we were talking about a song that wasn't just your ordinary rock song. It was something else altogether."

The band's performance of "Smells Like Teen Spirit" that day was subpar by any technical standard: Cobain didn't play the first notes of the introduction, and the microphone in front of him kept slipping from its stand. Eventually Kurt had to lean down and crane his neck as low as possible, because the microphone was pointing at the ground and was parallel to his stomach. Mercifully, an audience member stepped forward and held the microphone steady for the rest of the song. But Nirvana was never a band that aspired to play technically perfect music. They sought to capture the passion behind the song rather than hit every note. "Punk rock should mean freedom," Cobain would tell a French television station six months later. "It means playing whatever you want as sloppy as you want as long as it's good and has passion."

The band had debuted "Smells Like Teen Spirit" in Seattle at a surprise show six months earlier at the O.K. Hotel. That first performance got the audience jumping up and down, but the tune still wasn't honed enough at that point to make the room explode. But by the time of the Beehive in-store, the song hit the room like a hurricane. "When they played 'Smells Like Teen Spirit,'" says Jamie Brown, "the crowd went completely and totally nuts. You could see the stars in the eyes of the kids. By that point, by that day, Nirvana had already broken Seattle. As of that moment, they were superstars in Seattle. They had changed the lives of those kids. These kids had gotten there early and staked out their places, and on that day their lives had been forever changed by this band. For some of the older people, it wasn't that easy because their brains got involved."

Forty-five minutes after they began, the band put down their instruments, walked into the crowd, and began to sign copies of the CD, which is usually the only activity that happens at in-store record release parties. A little after 8 P.M. on September 16, 1991, Seattle teenagers walked into the darkening night holding the first copies of Nevermind to be sold, emblazoned with autographs from Kurt, Krist, and Dave.

IN BLOOM

In May 1991, producer Butch Vig sat behind the recording console at Sound City Studios in Van Nuys, California, adjusting his volume control to what he describes as a level called "stun." It was the first time Vig had ever worked in a large studio, and one of the few times he'd ever recorded any project outside the confines of his own Madison, Wisconsin, recording facility, Smart Studios. The thirty-five-year-old Vig had just finished recording the new Smashing Pumpkins album, *Gish,* at Smart, but now he found himself called in at the eleventh hour to record a major-label album. Though Vig's résumé already included forty-eight different independent albums prior to *Nevermind*, this was to be his first major-label credit. Once he'd set his levels at stun, Vig stood behind the studio glass observing Kurt Cobain, Dave Grohl, and Krist Novoselic, collectively Nirvana. The trio was attempting another take of the song "Lithium."

Nirvana were recording the album for DGC, a label many in the industry referred to as the "punk" arm of Geffen Records. Geffen had beaten out numerous other labels and had recently purchased the contract rights of Nirvana from the Seattle-based independent label Sub Pop for a reported $75,000 cash and a potential share of the profits from *Nevermind* if the album's sales exceeded two hundred thousand units. Nirvana's 1989 inaugural release, *Bleach*, on Sub Pop, had been produced for the tidy sum of $606.17 and had sold a considerable amount for an alternative rock band—it was Sub Pop's biggest-selling title at the time. Other than Nirvana, Sub Pop was best known for a roster that included Mudhoney, the Afghan Whigs, and Tad—all bands with tremendous critical reputations but with modest sales. At the time Nirvana was

the closest thing to a pop band on Sub Pop's roster, and a few major labels had tried to buy the entire indie label just to sign Nirvana. With new songs, major-label distribution, and lengthy touring, most insiders expected sales of *Nevermind* to reach a respectable one hundred thousand units, which, by the standards set in alternative rock at the time, would have been a big hit. Sales of *Nevermind* would, in fact, eventually surpass ten million copies worldwide.

Vig recalls the sessions for *Nevermind* as being laid-back, without high expectations. "They had a kind of casual attitude toward making the record," he says. "There was not a lot of pressure. *I* felt more pressure making that record than they did, because it was really the first major-label record I was making."

Nirvana had been trying to track a live-in-the-studio take of "Lithium," a song that already was being talked about as potentially the first hit from the album. However, the session was not coming along easily. The mood in studio A that afternoon was relaxed as the session began, but as the day progressed the atmosphere started to tighten up. As yet another take for "Lithium" got under way, the third attempt of the day, it

Here we are now: Kurt Cobain, Krist Novoselic, and Dave Grohl. (PHOTOGRAPH BY ED SIRRS/RETNA)

became clear to the band that this one was *not* a keeper. The band basically gave up and did what they usually did whenever a studio session wasn't going well: they started jamming, a process that had marked most of their songwriting and rehearsal efforts in the past. For *Bleach,* their studio time had been so limited that they'd rehearsed for two solid weeks before going near the studio. Whenever those rehearsals would break down, the band would jam on something they could easily play, to build up their confidence level again.

"We would always break into stuff like the 'Lithium' jam," bassist Krist Novoselic recalls. "Sometimes at rehearsal we wouldn't even go into the set, we'd just play stuff like [that jam]. We might even play something like that for the whole rehearsal, mostly just to get stuff out of our systems. So that day, we just started busting into that. It was really about trying to find a groove. We were trying to make this wall of noise and to turn it into something."

Though "Lithium" was over for the moment, Vig had the foresight to keep the tapes rolling. The band continued to jam, churn, and thrash on one of their rehearsal grooves. But this time around, the jamming was having the opposite effect from what it usually accomplished—rather than giving the band more confidence to help them move on and eventually tackle the song again, it was enraging Cobain. He began to lose his patience as Grohl and Novoselic continued to play. A volcanic musical reaction was about to spew forth in the studio, and this unexpected eruption was captured live on the session tape.

Vig watched all this from his control booth, looking down on the scene with amazement, listening to the noise blasting through the studio monitors. Six minutes and twenty seconds into the jam, in a ferocious orgasmic explosion, Cobain pulled his guitar high overhead and smashed his left-handed Mosrite in anger, screaming out a bloodcurdling cry of frustration.

"Kurt got so into it that day that he smashed his guitar," remembers Novoselic. "There was nobody there—no audience or anything. Kurt was in a trance or something. He just flipped out and broke his guitar."

In shock, Vig continued to roll the tape, capturing even the last sounds of feedback noise dying out. It was to be the last song the band would cut that day, as everyone present thought it might be best to end the session early. Though the day had come to an apocalyptic ending, this aborted jam would end up as the "hidden track" on *Nevermind,* sonically buried at the end of the CD. The track would come to be known as "Endless, Nameless."

The electricity that shot through the mixing console that day is reflected in Vig's eyes as he recalls the *Nevermind* sessions. "Kurt didn't have much patience," Vig remembers, "but there was a ton of passion to *Nevermind.* And a lot of it boiled down to Kurt's vocal performance and the persona you got from his voice." And the other significant thing that Vig observed Nirvana's craft of songwriting: "They wrote killer songs. I know that Kurt was always really leery about his pop sensibility, but I totally encouraged it."

It was not, however, pop music that Cobain created that day at Sound City, because "Endless, Nameless" is nothing if not a punk anthem: a deconstruction of the rock song replacing any crafting of melody. Vig remembers being the last person in the studio that night— he'd gone back to listen to the day's work and to fill out his tracking sheets—and he recalls looking out from the control room into the large studio. Sitting in the middle of the room, highlighted by the spotlights that were set to illuminate the band members, was Kurt's smashed guitar. For *Nevermind,* the album that would go on to smash all sales records for a debut major-label release, it would be a good omen. For Nirvana, the lengthy historical trip—from chance encounter; high school bands; weeks of rehearsal above a beauty salon; a revolving-door drummer saga; to pop stardom—was approaching its zenith. When Cobain smashed his left-handed Mosrite that day, it wasn't just the frustration of recording "Lithium" that surged up in him: it was the frustration of years of bitter struggle, personal turmoil, and bone-crushing demoralization that had begun two decades earlier in Aberdeen, Washington.

BREED

Aberdeen, Washington, was a strange place to serve as the breeding ground for what would become the defining band of a generation, but then all great albums come from unusual confines, from the margins of society rather than from the hub. The most influential band of the '60s, the Beatles, came from Liverpool, which, in a way, is the Aberdeen, Washington, of the United Kingdom. Like Aberdeen, it was a place that time forgot, where economic struggle was a part of daily existence and blue-collar workers were the norm. The most potent record of the '70s, the Sex Pistols' epochal *Never Mind the Bollocks,* was from a band that lived in London, where the postimperial youth culture produced its own marginalized culture. And though the '80s may not have provided any singular album that so changed music, it did serve as an incubation period for a number of U.S. bands hailing from the East and Midwest who created a music underground on small independently owned labels. These bands—including Sonic Youth, Killdozer, Hüsker Dü, R.E.M., Soul Asylum, Smashing Pumpkins, and the Replacements—began to modify the punk sound that had come out of England in the late '70s and to transform it into their own alterna-rock universe. Artistically, *Nevermind* would combine the pop sensibilities of the Beatles with the punk aesthetic the Sex Pistols offered up on *Never Mind the Bollocks.* It would be no small irony that the greatest rock 'n' roll album of the '90s would share part of a title with the Sex Pistols' long player.

But the members of Nirvana looked not only to the Beatles and the Sex Pistols as influences; they also looked in their own backyard. The

Nirvana 1989: Chad Channing, Krist Novoselic, and Kurt Cobain.
(PHOTOGRAPH BY ALICE WHEELER)

Northwest region had already seen a small musical explosion of its own in the late '50s and early '60s when bands like the Wailers, the Sonics, and the Kingsmen had invented the original grunge sound popularized by "Louie, Louie." Though the first wave of what locals call "the original Northwest sound" had met with limited commercial success (the exception being the Kingsmen's hit single "Louie, Louie," which went as high as Number 2 on the *Billboard* charts), these pioneering bands did have a tremendous impact on the local music scene. Two decades later Mudhoney, the Melvins, and Nirvana would discover these homegrown releases in used-record bins and be influenced by the raw, Northwest, protopunk sound.

"The connection that I see between Nirvana and the Sonics and Wailers is an appreciation for noise," says Peter Blecha, curator at the Experience Music Project. "While other bands in the early to mid-'60s—specifically Jan and Dean and the Beach Boys—were attempting to get pure and clean sounds, the garage bands of that era from the Northwest were heading in the opposite direction. You had the Sonics up here slitting their speakers or poking them with pencils to get that ratty-sounding distortion. That was really one of the beginnings of an appreciation for distortion and noise-making, and it was a central thread that linked the two generations." Blecha says that Courtney Love told him that Cobain's record collection included numerous albums by the Sonics, Wailers, and Galaxies, along with copies of *The Rocket*, the Northwest music magazine that wrote about both the region's current groups and its musical history. "By listening to those records and reading about it in those magazines, Kurt must have picked up some respect for local and regional traditions," Blecha speculates.

The same geographic factors that helped isolate the Northwest culturally helped spawn the second Northwest musical explosion in the late '80s. One of the reasons cited most often by Seattleites for forming their own bands was simply the lack of concerts for them to attend: both Seattle and Portland are so far away from any other large metropolitan cities that most underground bands didn't include the Northwest on their tour itineraries. When a few national bands took the risk of long drives from San Francisco or Minneapolis—groups like Hüsker Dü, Black Flag, and the Avengers—they found enthusiastic audiences and packed houses.

It was on one of those rare tours of the Northwest by Black Flag that Kurt Cobain had his first exposure to live punk rock. It was a concert that changed his life. In interviews through the years, Cobain told journalists that he sold his record collection (which included albums by groups like Foreigner, Pat Benatar, and Journey) to buy the twelve-dollar ticket. It was worth every penny to Cobain, who was only seventeen years old at the time of the Black Flag show. "It was really great," he later told Michael Azerrad. "I was instantly converted." This single, fundamental moment in Kurt's life seemed to cement his love for music, already infused with influences from pop and hard rock, into a love for punk rock. He would struggle with this triple collision of musical genres throughout his professional career.

Cobain was born on February 20, 1967, and grew up in three towns in the western part of Washington: Aberdeen, Hoquiam, and Montesano. In an early, self-penned bio sheet for Nirvana, he described the band as being "spawned from the bowels of a redneck loser town called Aberdeen, WA." His memories of his hometown were anything but sentimental.

Aberdeen was a ready-made punk rock laboratory simply because it was so marginalized and so far outside of society's mainstream. It resembles more the vision of small-town America created in David Lynch's fictional *Twin Peaks* than it does a Norman Rockwell diorama. Set in a place that many might consider one of the most scenic in the nation—on a plain where mountains, a forest, a river, and a great ocean harbor meet—the city is a perfect proof that things are not always the way they seem. The picturesque landscape has been decimated by years of fueling the economy with natural resources. It sits in one of the most heavily logged regions in the world, with huge clear-cuts visible on any of the major routes into town. Though most forest service companies have limited the practice of clear-cutting in the past decade, there are still huge swaths of what was once prime forest now covering southwest Washington with a sea of stumps. Cobain described Aberdeen to *Monk* magazine as "a very small community with a lot of people who have very small minds. Basically if you're not prepared to join the logging industry, you're going to be beaten up or run out of town."

Logging is to Aberdeen what the mill was to the prototypical mill town on the eastern seaboard of the United States in the early twentieth

The house in Aberdeen that Kurt Cobain grew up in.
(PHOTOGRAPH BY CHRIS PHILLIPS)

During the winter of 1985, Kurt Cobain spent some nights under the North Aberdeen bridge, just blocks from his mother's house.

century. But while most of those early mill towns have found other industries to replace the mills' original purpose, Aberdeen's entire history has been dominated by logging. The town hit its peak population in 1930 when it boasted twenty-two thousand residents, and there has been a slow but steady decline ever since. Not only did the residents of Aberdeen leave when opportunity presented itself; the town continued to lose jobs, wealth, and its own sense of community.

It was a perfect place to breed rebels. In a 1992 interview with a British newspaper, Cobain described the band's early experience in their hometown: "Well, they started out as these little fuck-ups in a small town from Aberdeen. All they did was smoke pot and spray-paint the walls. They were all rebellious and didn't mind their parents. And they had to find a new outlet for all their rebellious energy, so they started a band."

That band came about when Cobain met Krist Novoselic during high school in the mid-'80s. Krist was born in 1965 in Compton, California, but his family had moved to Aberdeen by 1979—ironically, his father had found work there. The six-foot, seven-inch Novoselic grew up listening to the music of Led Zeppelin, Devo, Black Sabbath, and Aerosmith—in other words, he had the same influences as every other teenager from Aberdeen. But unlike most of his classmates, he also had the desire to create his own music. He picked up the guitar at the age of seventeen and took a few lessons from the same teacher who had briefly instructed Cobain. He even began to dabble in the blues—until he came under the influence of Buzz Osborne.

Osborne, a member of the Aberdeen band the Melvins, introduced Krist and Kurt and played a role as the unofficial organizer of the Aberdeen music scene. Everyone knew who he was, and he was responsible for many of the introductions that would lead to the formation of some of the area's most influential bands. Novoselic recalled Osborne's musical influence in an interview with an Australian radio station in 1992: "He discovered punk rock. And he was turning people on to it. I heard it and it sounded live to me. And I borrowed the record *Album—Generic Flipper* [by the band Flipper] and I listened to it." The record changed Novoselic's life and give him a new focus. "It was like a revelation," Novoselic says today, echoing a description others would apply to describe their own experience with Nirvana's music. "It changed my whole approach to life. Buzz was the preacher and his gospel was punk rock." Osborne introduced both Kurt and Krist to the hard-core punk music of groups like Black Flag, Flipper, the Butthole Surfers, and the Circle Jerks.

In the few interviews he's done about his early roots, Osborne himself always downplays his role in the scene and says his other contemporaries turned him on to the larger punk arena. "A couple of guys in high school who were quite a bit older than me were into the Clash," Osborne told *The Rocket* in August 1993. "They saw the Clash in Seattle once on a laugh, and said it was the most insane thing they'd ever seen. I kind of got interested. I liked all the really heavy stuff at the time: Nugent, Aerosmith, Kiss, Black Sabbath, AC/DC . . . all the fourteen-year-old heavy-metal kid stuff. At the same time, I was into David Bowie really heavily, which was very odd. I didn't know anyone else who was into it. Then I met this guy who had moved to Seattle and had joined the Lewd, moved to San Francisco, and now was moving back to Aberdeen; why, I don't know. He had an immense collection of punk rock records and it was a really good education. I never would have found those records; none of that stuff was ever down there." In some ways it was the very dearth of punk records and live shows that helped Aberdeen become a breeding ground: any punk album that made its way to Aberdeen was passed around like holy scripture and listened to with far more attention than it got in the big city.

As Cobain and Novoselic traveled in the Melvins' social circle, they began to get to know each other. During this time, Kurt made a tape of his own original music with help from Dale Crover of the Melvins. Novoselic continued the story for *Nevermind: It's an Interview,* a promotional CD Geffen released in 1992 that contained extensive interviews with the band done by Kurt St. Thomas: "One of the songs on it was 'Spank Thru,'" Novoselic told St. Thomas. "And [Buzz] turned me on to it and I really liked it. It kind of got me excited. So I said [to Kurt], 'Hey man, let's start a band.' We scrounged up a drummer and we started practicing. We took it very seriously, too." The thrashing, hard-driving passion of punk music seemed to focus and unite the two young men.

When Cobain and Novoselic first came together, they played mostly cover tunes. One of the first bands they formed was a country-rock group, the Sellouts. They also played Creedence Clearwater Revival covers. Not unlike other teenage bands, the names they played under—along with the styles of their music—would continue to change and evolve until they hit upon the moniker Nirvana almost two years later. Some of the pre-Nirvana names they used included Ted-Ed-Fred, Pen Cap Chew, the Stiff Woodies, the Throat Oysters, and Bliss.

Although two-thirds of the future Nirvana were in place by 1987, they continued to search for that crucial yet elusive element of a good drummer who could anchor their sound. In the fall of 1987, Kurt placed an ad in *The Rocket* that read: "SERIOUS DRUMMER WANTED. Underground attitude, Black Flag, Melvins, Zeppelin, Scratch Acid, Ethel Merman. Versatile as heck. Kurdt" (Cobain spelled both his first and last names differently throughout his career). The search for a drummer haunted Kurt and Krist for the next three years. They used their various drummers as time markers along the way, and when Kurt described the history of the band to a journalist in 1990, it was the drummers that dominated his history lesson: "So they started a band with a drummer. Then they kicked that drummer out. Then they got another drummer. Then they kicked that drummer out. Then they got another drummer. Then they kicked that drummer out. Then they made a record with that drummer. Then they kicked him out. And then they got another one. And then they borrowed one from the Melvins, this guy named Dale and then he couldn't stay. And they got another one and then they kicked him out." It would be several years before the band would find the final missing link, a developmental journey that mirrored bands like the Beatles, the Who, and the New York Dolls, all of whom came together only after finding the right drummer.

In 1988, yet another drummer had exited the band's revolving door, leaving a temporary vacancy behind the drum kit. As per Kurt's history lesson, Nirvana enlisted longtime friend and Melvins' drummer Dale Crover to help them record a formal demo at Seattle's Reciprocal Studios on January 23, 1988. It would be their first studio session. At the time, producer Jack Endino was recording a number of up-and-coming Northwest bands, including Green River (who later evolved into Mudhoney and Mother Love Bone, the latter mutating into Pearl Jam) and Soundgarden. Endino recorded some ten tracks by Nirvana: "Floyd the Barber," "Paper Cuts," "Downer," "Hairspray Queen," "If You Must," "Pen Cap Chew," "Spank Thru," "Beeswax," "Mexican Seafood," and "Aero Zeppelin." Novoselic would recall the session as a productive one for *Nevermind: It's an Interview:* "We jammed for about a week, made some songs and put together this tape. . . . And a couple of those songs made it over to the *Bleach* LP." The entire session lasted a reported six hours, including recording and mixing. The total cost for Endino's work was a mere $152.44. Endino gave a mix of the tracks to Jonathan Poneman, who had recently cofounded a fledgling independent record label with partner Bruce Pavitt.

Back in 1986, Pavitt and Poneman had begun a label they called Sub Pop. At the time, Pavitt was an employee of the Muzak Corporation, where he worked coordinating tapes and programming. More important-ly, in Muzak's shipping room he came in contact with many members of Seattle bands. He was in many ways a visionary who theorized that regionalism was the driving force keeping American pop music alive. He enthusiastically supported the Seattle rock scene by starting up a local fanzine titled *Subterranean Pop,* which he eventually shortened to *Sub Pop;* by writing a column in *The Rocket* under that name; and by even-tually putting out cassettes that accompanied his fanzine. Poneman, for his part, was a musician in several Seattle bands (including the Tree Climbers), but also a successful booker and promoter. Though neither of the partners had much business experience, Poneman was a smooth talker and gave the impression that he was a skilled businessman. After spending about twenty thousand dollars to start up Sub Pop (named after

Pavitt's fanzine), the company began its operations on a scanty budget, carefully tiptoeing on the thin ice of solvency.

Though their lack of business acumen would prove to be a perennial problem, the pair did exhibit something close to genius when it came to marketing. One of their shrewdest concepts was the Sub Pop Singles Club, a subscription service where collectors received a new limited-edition 45 rpm, seven-inch vinyl record each month. When you signed up for the club, you were essentially guaranteeing that you'd buy whatever Poneman and Pavitt decided to issue over the next year. The label had already established a national reputation based on their early roster of talent, which included, among others, Soundgarden, Mudhoney, Tad, and the Fluid. They decided that the first edition of their Singles Club would be a release by an up-and-coming band named Nirvana doing "Love Buzz." This simple decision in and of itself may have been a turning point for the group: at that time the band was not well known, and their debut single (a cover song) could have bombed. As it was, the sheer number of subscribers to the Singles Club guaranteed that a large audience would hear this band, and many of them may not otherwise have gambled and bought an individual single by an unknown band.

While Sub Pop had been gearing up, Nirvana had been struggling to find a new drummer to replace Dave Foster, who had followed Crover into the drummer's seat. They placed another ad in the March 1988 issue of *The Rocket:* "DRUMMER WANTED. Play hard, sometimes light, underground, versatile, fast, medium, slow, versatile, serious, heavy, versatile, dorky, nirvana, hungry. Kurdt 352-0992." The phone number was for Kurt's apartment in Olympia; by that point he'd moved in with his girlfriend there, while Novoselic had moved to Tacoma. Little did Kurt and Krist realize that these criteria (with the possible exception of "dorky") would so accurately describe their future drummer for *Nevermind*. Again, the ad was unsuccessful.

In the spring of 1988, Novoselic and Cobain had the fortune to meet their fourth drummer, one who would greatly influence their music. Chad Channing was playing in a band called Tick-Dolly-Row in a Tacoma club on the same bill with Bliss, the name Nirvana was going by at the time. Channing says that when he saw Bliss that night he honestly thought "they sucked. It was really, really loose and really, really noisy. The sound was bad in that hall, but the drummer at that time, Dave Foster, wasn't hitting that well. He was doing a lot of Bonham-type fills, quads and triplets. It was this wall of weird noise that kind of made sense sometimes."

Channing was impressed with a few things about the show: Cobain was wearing some flashy pants, the bass player was really tall, and, despite the poor sound, there was something about the band's attitude that he found infectious. "It was very distorted and very unclear," he says. "But it was kind of cool at the same time. It was obvious that these guys didn't give a fuck whether they were cool. But it was nothing impressive."

Despite that initial meeting, Channing was intrigued enough that when the band asked him to jam with them a few weeks later, he took them up on the offer and began to practice with them. He played his first show with the group in May 1988 at a club called the Vogue in Seattle. He says that neither Kurt nor Krist ever told him he'd been appointed the new drummer.

Three months later the band recorded their first single, "Love Buzz"—a cover of the Shocking Blue song—backed with "Big Cheese," a song written about Poneman. It was produced in a limited-edition run of one thousand copies for the Sub Pop Singles Club. With a 45 out, the band began to tour ("Even though in most places no one knew who we were," Channing recalls) and to talk about doing a full-length album. They signed a contract with Sub Pop and began writing the songs for their debut LP. It, too, would be recorded with Endino at Reciprocal, in December 1988. The *Bleach* sessions were very quick—four days of recording—but set a pattern of accident and happenstance that would mirror the band's future recording sessions. On the first day, Endino remembers that the band mistakenly tuned their guitars too low, which helped further the deep sound of the songs. "They tuned down to even lower than they usually tuned," Endino recalls. "I never asked them to tune down. ['Blew'] was in D, but they tuned down to C. The strings usually go out of tune at that point. The bass is so low. It's way down there. As I remember, it was just an experiment." Though the band recorded four or five songs that day, Endino says all of them sounded awful other than "Blew," which had benefited by the tuning mistake.

"We had tuned down to D to record 'Swap Meet,'" recalls Channing, "and we went on to 'Blew.' We tuned down to D for that song, but we'd already tuned down to D and we went down and tuned a step lower, thinking we hadn't tuned down already. So they actually were in C, which is so low on a bass guitar that the string should have been slapping. For some reason it didn't slap. If it would have slapped, then we might have realized what had happened and we might have gone back and recorded it properly. We realized it after we cut it. Jack said, 'That seems really low. Are you guys sure you tuned down to D?' And we checked it and went, 'Oh, man, we are down in C.' And we asked Jack, 'Should we do the song over?' And he said, 'Nah, let's keep it.'"

Bleach came out in June 1989. At the time, Sub Pop's promotional publicity for the album humorously hyped the band: "Hypnotic and righteous heaviness from these Olympia pop stars. They're young, they own their own van, and they're going to make us rich!" Prophetic words indeed. The vinyl LP sold well for a small indie release at forty-thousand-plus copies, which for an album not available on CD was a huge sale (vinyl buyers also tended to be the kind of taste-makers that influenced others). Nirvana followed up *Bleach* with an EP for Sub Pop, recorded in the fall of 1989, titled "Blew." It was released in December 1989, and for Nirvana marked not only the end of the '80s, but the beginning of the next stage of their development, leading inevitably to *Nevermind*.

COME AS YOU ARE

It was the second day of April 1990, and the three members of Nirvana—at that time Cobain, Novoselic, and Channing—drove into Madison, Wisconsin, in their white Dodge van, with a sense of elation. They were there to record what was planned to be their second full album on Sub Pop. The band settled into their accommodations at the Edgewater Hotel, overlooking Madison's beautiful Lake Mendota, but there would be little sightseeing; most of their time in Madison would be spent in the studio or writing songs. Kurt had written a handful of songs prior to his arrival in Madison, but he continued to work on the material once they arrived and had time for little else. Later that day, the band made their way over to the first meeting with Butch Vig.

Vig himself had begun in the music industry as a drummer for the midwest band Spooner in the early 1980s. After a couple of near misses at the big time—the band was well reviewed but their records sold poorly—Spooner mutated into Fire Town later in the decade. Vig found himself in a band with a hit when MTV began to play Fire Town's video "Carry the Torch" in regular rotation. Fire Town made two albums for Atlantic, and Vig had his first taste of the major-label record business.

Vig's own musical interests extended beyond his bands. While at the University of Wisconsin at Madison, he pursued a degree in Communication Arts and Film, which led him into making experimental soundtrack music for his fellow classmates. He recalls the sound collage work and the impact it had on him: "It just encouraged me to try to make interesting sound recordings and deal with the kind of environment you have." He began dabbling with synthesizers, old analog equipment, and

Butch Vig and Doug Olson working at Smart Studios' control board in spring 1990.
(Photograph courtesy Smart Studios)

sound effects. He began to produce, a process he best describes as "pushing the buttons and making the decisions."

In 1980, Smart Studios was born in the Madison home of Butch's business partner and longtime friend, Steve Marker. Marker, who had met Vig at the University of Wisconsin, set up a four-track tape recorder in his basement. "That is actually where the original studio idea came from," Vig remembers. At the time, Vig and Marker were more interested in experimentation than creating a commercial recording studio. "We spent a lot of time recording all kinds of strange, cool sounds," Vig adds.

By 1983, after Marker and Vig pooled their meager savings and sold an old guitar, Smart Studios had moved into a warehouse space called the Gisholt building. "We scraped up enough money to buy an eight-track, which seemed like a lot of money. I think it was $2,200," says Vig. "We bought a couple more microphones. We really didn't have anything at all in the way of gear, but we would approach bands and say, 'Hey look, do you want to come to our studio and record some of your material?'" They began to record local and regional punk bands for ten dollars an hour. Some of their early projects included Bitter Pleasures, Tar Babies, and Killdozer. By reinvesting all their earnings into Smart, Vig and Marker were able to expand the business, upgrade equipment, and move into their present location in 1987.

Out-of-towners would be hard pressed to locate or even notice the two-story redbrick building which stands in the elongated shadow of Wisconsin's State Capitol on Madison's east side. Madison itself is a unique city of two hundred thousand residents located about 150 miles northwest of Chicago, Illinois, an urban oasis in the middle of miles of dairy farms. In that it combines the diverse elements of a major college and the state capitol, it isn't all that different from Olympia, Washington. Smart Studios even looks like it would fit into the Olympia cityscape, housed in a simple old brick building, plopped into a district zoned for both residential and commercial use. The entire set of first-floor windows is tightly sealed to keep out the busy street noises and to keep in the music. The east-side neighborhood contains dozens of old two-story homes that form a semicircle around the studio, and all share a spectacular view of the capitol. Though the studio looked nondescript on the outside, inside Vig and Marker continued to upgrade their facility—first to a sixteen-track and later to twenty-four-track with digital and sampling capabilities. By the time of the Nirvana sessions, it was one of the most advanced recording facilities in Madison.

By concentrating on recording bands he liked rather than seeking big budgets, Vig had established a reputation for himself as a top independent producer of raw and raucous underground records. Though none of his early punk productions sold particularly well, they were being listened to by the likes of Sonic Youth's Thurston Moore and by Kurt Cobain. Vig's popularity as a producer stemmed from his ability to translate an artist's ferocious sonic vision into a clean, honest documentary form, buoyed by his laid-back nature and experience as a musician. "In Spooner, the first producer we worked with was Gary Klebe from Shoes, who paid a lot of attention to detail," explains Vig. "And [working with Klebe] rubbed off on me. I understood what it takes—you take extra time and move the microphone around or listen to it in the context of the gui-

NIRVANA

SUB POP RECORDS
1932 - 1st Ave., Suite 1103
Seattle, WA 98101
(206) 441-8441

Terminal Booking:
(206) 441-3011

photo: Charles Peterson

The official Sub Pop promo photo from the time of Bleach, shot by Charles Peterson.
(PHOTOGRAPH COURTESY EXPERIENCE MUSIC PROJECT)

tars and the EQ, or whatever you're doing, and try and give the instruments more space or separation. Even working on crummy gear with a band that couldn't play together, I still wanted it to sound good."

It was Vig's reputation for getting the best out of relatively obscure underground acts for record labels such as Touch and Go, Flaming Pie, Twin/Tone, and Amphetamine Reptile that brought him to the attention of

Sub Pop's Jonathan Poneman. Prior to Nirvana, Sub Pop had hired Vig to produce a record with Smashing Pumpkins (the single "La Dolly Vita" backed with "Tristessa"). After hearing Vig's 1989 production of *12 Point Buck* by Killdozer, Poneman called Vig to propose that he record an album with Sub Pop's Nirvana at Smart Studios. Butch recalls Poneman's enthusiasm for Nirvana and his desire to reproduce Vig's trademark sound for the band. "Jonathan called up because he said he loved the sound of this Killdozer record, and he said, 'I want you to get that sound for Nirvana.'" Butch was well aware of Sub Pop's reputation in the indie world, and he remembers thinking, "I wanted to work with Sub Pop because I knew they were a cool label."

Novoselic confirms that it was Poneman who first suggested Vig but says he and Cobain were well aware of Vig's productions. "Jonathan recommended him," Novoselic recalls. "And Butch had just recorded Tad, which we knew about, and that crazy band Killdozer, where they'd done Neil Diamond covers and stuff." The members of Nirvana were always good friends with the members of Tad, and since Vig had gotten Tad's approval, Novoselic and Cobain thought they'd give Vig a try too. "It just seemed like the thing to do," Novoselic says.

Madison's die-hard ice fishermen were still camped out on the thin ice of Lake Mendota when the members of Nirvana found their way to Smart Studios on a cold April Monday in 1990. The band didn't have the luxury of time on their side. They had just played a show the night before at Chicago's premier post-punk palace, Cabaret Metro, and driven until 3 A.M. to reach their Madison hotel. With another live date looming on April 10 in Ann Arbor, the band had from the second of April through the sixth—exactly five days—to get to know their new producer and track some new songs. Nirvana wanted to quickly set down a number of newly penned originals in the same vein as their punk-rock predecessors. They were seeking a recording process they knew well—down and dirty.

The session could last only a work week because Sub Pop had scheduled the band for an eight-week tour of the United States, and with virtually no tour support, the band needed to play as many shows as possible to pay for such essentials as gas and food. Krist Novoselic related the game plan the band had going into the Smart session on *Nevermind: It's an Interview:* "Everything was geared up to put out this second Nirvana record. We were going to record maybe a few more songs in

Seattle. This was going to be on Sub Pop." Novoselic's assertion that the album was planned as their next Sub Pop release is important because their motives would be questioned later when the band began negotiating with other labels and seeking relief from their Sub Pop contract.

Chad Channing also remembers that the band went into the Madison sessions convinced that they were going to record most of their second album that week and that it was indeed going to be released on Sub Pop. Unlike *Bleach*, where the band had had two solid weeks of rehearsal before going into the studio, this time Nirvana had been forced to work out most of their songs on the road. "We used sound checks and the shows themselves to work on new songs," Channing says. "We had a bunch of great new songs, though Kurt was nervous because a lot of them weren't finished." Cobain's habit of writing songs in the studio continued through Nirvana's entire career. Many of the band's best songs were worked out while the studio clock was running.

When Nirvana arrived at the unmarked side street entrance to Smart, they immediately found themselves inside the studio's office. A quick left turn ushered them into the studio A control room. There, in the dimly lit room, they found Butch Vig preparing for the session. Engineer Doug Olson was also present to help out Butch and the band as needed. Walking past the mixing board, the band entered a doorway to the cozy studio to set up their own gear. Smart wasn't a big studio, but compared to Reciprocal, the tiny Seattle studio where the band had recorded *Bleach*, it was cavernous.

Vig recalls the first day: "When they showed up, they were actually very funny and charming, particularly Krist. Kurt was very charming when he came, and then he would get really moody and sit in the corner and not talk for forty-five minutes." Channing remembers the band's mood as being very upbeat, and Kurt put his usual prankster antics on hold. He says the group tackled the sessions with all the seriousness they had applied to making their first album, *Bleach*. "It was a big deal to us to actually be able to record another album," he says. "It was a *really* big deal."

As the band got used to the relaxed surroundings of Smart, Novoselic took the lead in checking out Vig's punk-rock pedigree. He quizzed Vig on his personal music interests and was particularly concerned about the recording process. Krist soon realized that Butch shared Nirvana's musical philosophy. "He asked me about a lot of punk records, asked me if I could get this or that kind of sound," Vig remembers. "They didn't want to sound too clean or trebly; they wanted to sound *real* heavy." For his part, Vig also checked out the band: though he'd heard *Bleach*, demos, and live tapes before producing the Smart sessions, Vig had yet to see the band play live.

From the start of the session, Cobain remained fairly quiet, letting Novoselic do much of the talking, while Channing took direction from the other two members of the band. Engineer Olson was serving as an assistant to Vig at the time. "Smart was very informal then," Olson recalls. "I was not called an assistant engineer, although technically that's probably what I was doing." Olson helped set up mike positions and moved equipment around at the early stages of the session. He modestly underscores his involvement: "I don't want to overestimate my contribution to the way those [recordings] sound. Butch is quite an open-minded guy, so the environment, if someone is working with him, is generally one open to suggestions."

Most of the basic song arrangements were complete by the time Nirvana came to record at Smart, though Channing says that some of them still needed lyrical work, and the band was unsure of what songs to cut. "It took a while to get going," the drummer recalls. "I think at this particular session, it was slower trying to get the sounds together. Some of the

Smart Studios is located in a Madison neighborhood near the state capitol. (PHOTOGRAPH BY JIM BERKENSTADT)

songs weren't even completely finished. Some of them were ideas we'd run through a couple of times and then we had to go on tour. There was a feeling of hesitancy, recording some of the songs, because of the 'not readiness' about them that Kurt had. And there was some apprehension about what songs to record. They were so different than *Bleach*—it was a drastic change."

That hesitancy wasn't as apparent to Vig, who remembers being impressed by how together the group seemed. "They had been playing some of the songs live before coming to Madison, and the arrangements were pretty focused," Vig says. Still, of the seven songs that the band cut during the Smart sessions, only five of them had been performed live before, and "In Bloom" had been played for the first time at their show the day before in Chicago.

According to Channing, all of the members of Nirvana were impressed with Vig's style in the studio, and an instant rapport was formed. "Vig had a lot more input of ideas than we'd had in the past," Channing recalls. "Instead of saying 'What do you guys want to do?' he was more apt to say, 'I've done this with these bands, let's try it.' Working with the drum sounds, for example, he'd bring up all kinds of ideas. There were a lot of situations where we were taking a longer route trying to get to where we wanted. If we wanted to get a big sound, he'd bring up a bunch of ideas. It was definitely more experimental, though I never felt him being overbearing." One of the things the band struggled with the most, according to Vig, was the drum sound. He noticed that neither Cobain nor Novoselic was shy about making suggestions to Channing, though the communication between Chad and Kurt wasn't always ideal. Being a drummer himself, Vig managed to help the two work together and to help Channing capture the "big sound" that the band wanted.

Vig contemplated how he could change the artificial recording environment to make the recordings of Nirvana match the fury and intensity they were known for from their live shows. He considered several ideas before improvising a unique experiment that might accomplish his sonic goal. "I put several sheets of plywood on the floor during tracking to make the room sound a little more live," he recalls. For the most part, the band used their own gear which they had brought with them, except a Fender Bassman that Vig got Cobain to use on "Lithium" and "In Bloom." Vig adds proudly, "We used my Yamaha snare drum on several songs, the same one that was also used on Smashing Pumpkins' *Gish*."

Doug Olson doesn't remember many details from the conversations that took place that week, but he was struck by Cobain's singular vision. Though a man of few words, Kurt knew what he wanted his music to sound like, and he approached recording with a self-assurance that few people working on their second album bring into the studio. During setup, it became apparent to Olson that Cobain was planning to use a transistorized amplifier for his guitar. "He had a Sunn guitar amp," Olson says. "I'm quite prejudiced against transistors and toward tubes in amplifiers for musical instruments. I hadn't even heard the amp at that point. I was just thinking in the back of my mind, 'Oh, we've got to set this guy up with a good tube amp so he can sound cool.' But, I didn't want to force anything on him." Olson diplomatically offered Cobain the use of his own classic Marshall tube amp sitting in Smart's basement equipment room. He distinctly recalls Cobain "looking at me with a very suspicious, slightly scowling look, saying, '*No*, I don't want to do that.'"

Olson's story highlights what others have observed about Kurt during Nirvana's Sub Pop era—he was a man torn between his punk ethos of rapidly recording lo-fi punk music and his love of a meticulous, tight-sounding pop song. "He was very conscious of that," says Olson. "It's hard to pin it down. I think he was probably a bundle of all kinds of contradictions." Meanwhile, Vig actively lobbied Cobain's pop-music side, telling Kurt, "You have a genius for doing this. Don't ignore it—it's beautiful." Vig admits, "I know that he felt self-conscious coming from a punk background and having these kind of gorgeously crafted rock songs. Even though his songs might have been kind of noisy, they still had really beautiful melodies and melodic structure."

Cobain stuck with the finely crafted pop songs, though for the Smart sessions he also used his transistor amp. The Smart sessions, far more than the *Nevermind* sessions that would follow, reflect the grungy, lo-fi sound that Nirvana attempted to capture with every live gig. Some still argue that the sound of the Smart sessions was far closer to what you heard from the band live than what you heard on any of their other recordings.

And like most things Nirvana, the sessions came and went quickly. Due to the short amount of time available before the band had to tour again, the tracks at Smart were recorded and mixed fast. Vig explains: "Most of the Sub Pop records I made we would do in a week. Record, track over two or three days, and then overdub a couple of days, and finish the vocals, and then mix two or three days." Nirvana's work at Smart followed this established pattern. During the five-day session the band recorded and finished six originals and one cover song: "Polly," "Pay to Play," "Dive," "In Bloom," "Sappy," "Lithium," and "Here She Comes Now."

THE SONGS: SMART SESSIONS

"Polly" is the only version of any song recorded at Smart Studios in 1990 that made it onto the final track lineup for *Nevermind*. Years later, pointing over his shoulder to the studio where Kurt recorded the song, Vig recalls the session: "Kurt just sat in there and did it on his acoustic guitar. We recorded 'Polly' here in half an hour flat. I just recorded it with an AKG 414 microphone."

"Polly" had been written by Kurt a couple of years earlier and the song had been in the band's live repertoire for the previous year. The version the band did live in 1989 was more often electric rather than the acoustic treatment it got at Smart. The song tells the harrowing true tale of a fourteen-year-old Tacoma, Washington, girl who was kidnapped on her way home from a concert. The lyrics describe in graphic, first-person detail the tortures that were inflicted on the girl before her eventual escape.

Taking the first-person perspective of the psychotic criminal in the song, though artistically interesting, probably confused some of Nirvana's fans and fueled the fire of its critics. Kurt often spoke out against macho men and rapists during the course of his career, no doubt a reaction to the logging bullies he had put up with back in his hometown. However, when people heard him sing about how Polly wanted water "to put out the blow torch," they had serious reservations concerning his graphic first-person portrayal.

Polly

An ad from the Madison *Isthmus* for the show Nirvana did while recording the Smart session.

33

In a 1992 interview with *Guitar World* magazine on the subject of "Polly," Kurt attempted to clarify the issue. "Just because I say 'I' in a song, it doesn't necessarily mean me," he explained. "A lot of people have a problem with that. It's just the way I write usually. Take on someone else's personality or character. I'd rather just use someone else's example, because, I don't know, my life is kind of boring. So, I just take stories from things that I've read and off the television. And stories I've heard and maybe even [from] some friends."

To record "Polly," Cobain used a cheap, out-of-tune, five-string acoustic guitar. Butch described it to journalist Alan Di Perna: "The strings were so old they didn't have any tone to them. A real plunky sound. It was the original strings. He never changed them." Cobain confirmed the guitar's history and explained why it sounded a bit flat on "Polly" in his 1992 *Guitar World* profile: "That's a twenty-dollar junk shop Stella [a brand of low-cost guitars]. I didn't bother changing the strings (laughs). In fact, I had to use duct tape to hold the tuning keys in place." Prior to recording, Kurt tuned the guitar a step and a half down from E.

Channing remembers that the song almost made it onto the "Blew" EP: "We almost thought about putting another version of that on that record. At that point the song was acoustic, but we played around with it, even did an electric version, and considered putting another version on the record."

Despite the guitar's condition, the studio take of "Polly" went quickly and sounded hauntingly beautiful. "'Polly' was recorded with Kurt and Krist playing live," explains Vig. "Then we went back after the guitars were finished and overdubbed vocals. Kurt sang harmonies with himself." The occasional cymbal accents, heard during dramatic pauses in the song, send shivers down the spine. "Chad overdubbed the cymbal crashes last," adds Butch.

One unique aspect of "Polly" was a vocal mistake made by Cobain during the master take. At about one minute and fifty seconds into the recording, Kurt comes in early, singing, "Polly said . . ." He stops abruptly, realizing he has entered early, and waits for the music to come around again before starting the verse over. This miscue is a nice touch that was never removed from the final master take. "We liked it," explains Vig, "and left it in. He actually did the same thing toward the end of 'Come As You Are' with the line, 'And I don't have a gun.'" Kurt would later retain the "Polly said" miscue when singing the song live in concert. Even the music books featuring transcriptions of the *Nevermind* album for guitar and piano retain this "mistake" in the official published lyrics.

All the Smart songs were recorded using a British-made twenty-five-by-sixteen-inch TAC Scorpion control board. "Polly" was recorded on 16-track, one-inch tape. It would sit untouched in Sub Pop's tape vault for another year, waiting to be placed on a Nirvana album. The song would not be resurrected until the *Nevermind* sessions. "'Polly' was an amazing song," admits Butch. "It blew me away when he sang it."

Pay to Play

This number would later evolve into "Stay Away" when the time came to record *Nevermind*. The song described Kurt's observations of people he felt were either corrupt or conformist. The lyrics to the song were unfinished at the time of the Smart sessions, but they provide some insight into emergent themes. Kurt sings, "Monkey see, monkey do / (I don't know why) / Walk around follow you / (I don't know why) / Do not keep it in / (I don't know why) / Rather have poison skin . . . (screams) Pay . . . Pay to play." The title also referred to a practice that was popular in clubs at the time: bands were given gigs only if they bought hundreds of tickets from the club, which they were then forced to sell on their own if they could. Though this practice wasn't common in the Northwest, the members of Nirvana were well aware of the Los Angeles scene where "pay to play" was standard at many clubs at the time.

Kurt's emerging songwriting skills were not lost on his producer. Vig told journalist Gillian Gaar, "Kurt's lyric writing was becoming more enigmatic. You weren't quite sure what he was singing about, but you knew it was really intense. I thought that his songwriting was just amazing."

Though the lyrics and title would change over the course of a year musically, the arrangement for "Pay to Play" was largely in place at the time of the Smart sessions. However, Chad Channing's percussion playing was another issue. Comparing the Smart version to its later counterpart on *Nevermind* demonstrates the differences in style of the two drummers: Grohl pounds the drums much harder. Perhaps the most interesting distinction of "Pay to Play" is the way in which the Smart version dissolves at the end into an extended feedback guitar jam. With a formal studio ending yet to be worked out at this point, Cobain leads with his searing guitar as the band improvises its musical exit. "Kurt was a good guitar player," remembers Olson of the session. "Not in a virtuoso Eddie Van Halen way. But he certainly could get the job done." This version of "Pay to Play," with the deconstructive ending, reflected the live performance nature of Nirvana—the group was a live band first and foremost that also happened to make records.

Note: though the Smart version of this song has been bootlegged over the years, it was later released commercially in 1994, as part of a DGC CD sampler entitled *DGC Rarities Volume 1.*

Dive

The song "Dive" was also finished by the band at Smart. Novoselic's bass playing is the highlight of the track. As rock's tallest bass player, Krist's guitar was slung down low, past his hip, to accommodate his long arms. The solo bass riff that leads into "Dive" seems reminiscent of the hook-y bass line running through Aerosmith's hit "Sweet Emotion." "We wrote that song together," Novoselic says. "He had that guitar riff and I added the bass riff, so I guess it just turned into a bass [driven] song."

"Dive" foreshadowed what Nirvana would achieve only a year later. Tightly composed, guitar-heavy hard pop, it was exactly the sort of song that pushed *Nevermind* up the charts. Strangely, though, the band left it off of *Nevermind*, and the Smart session track ended up as the B-side to "Sliver." Later, it was reprised on the *Incesticide* album (and eventually on the Sub Pop collection *The Grunge Years*). Kurt wrote in the liner notes for the Sub Pop anthology: "I'll be the first to admit that we're the '90s version of Cheap Trick or the Knack." "Dive" was always a crowd-pleasing song, and it would have been a perfect hit for Cheap Trick. Kurt had finally begun to create a magic formula by mixing heavy punk with pop hooks and harmonies.

In Bloom

"In Bloom" occupies the first slot on Smart Studios' archive copy of the unreleased Madison recording sessions. The musical arrangement and lyrics were finished when Nirvana began to record the song. Chad's drum part would remain basically the same a year later when Dave Grohl took over behind the kit, but Channing's jazzier drum fills stand in stark contrast to Grohl's hard-rock hits of a year later.

Novoselic says that originally there was another bridge within "In Bloom." "We recorded that song, and all the other songs at Smart, on sixteen-track," the bass player recalls. "And when we were listening to it, after we'd recorded it, we said, 'Ah, this bridge isn't that hot.' So Butch just took out a razor blade and cut the bridge out of the sixteen-track master, and then threw it in the garbage."

Remarkably, Cobain's vocal phrasing remained unchanged from the Smart performance to the *Nevermind* sessions. Kurt chose not to overdub a harmony vocal part while at Smart. This may have been more a factor of time and budget than aesthetics, though Novoselic says once the band nailed a song in the studio they rarely varied it. "Once we had a song down," he says, "we just always stuck with it. If it worked, why change it?"

The only real change to "In Bloom" when it was recorded at Sound City was an additional vocal track. Dave Grohl proved his flexibility, this time as a singer, by adding a harmony vocal overdub on top of Cobain's vocal for the track on *Nevermind*.

Kurt and Krist lead off "Sappy," strumming the opening chords that provide a repetitive structure for the song. Kurt's vocals come in after one melodic cycle, followed by the drums. The verse-chorus-verse-chorus composition of "Sappy" (the obvious reason it was originally called "Verse, Chorus, Verse") gives way to a fuzz guitar solo that dances around the song's melody. Though the thirty-five-second solo is very focused, it retains a spontaneous jam feel upon repeated listening. Nirvana would return to "Sappy" the following year for another attempt during the *Nevermind* sessions.

Sappy

The one cover song the band tackled during their stay at Smart was the Velvet Underground's classic "Here She Comes Now." Clocking in at just over five minutes in length, the song featured Kurt's repetition of the title and an interesting extended instrumental jam. The band played the song live at an Atlanta gig one month after the Smart sessions, and it occasionally showed up in their set lists for the next year. Channing says the song was one of the few that went easily at Smart, and that the session

Here She Comes Now

was somewhat lighthearted. "I was shocked we did that one," he remembers. "That was a fun song."

Novoselic says that the reason the band covered the song was because they'd been asked to by an indie label. "Gary from Tupelo Records called up and said he was putting out a Velvet Underground tribute record, and he wanted us to play on it. We had never played that song before [the Smart sessions] and we hardly ever played it after. We just kind of hashed it out. We did that song in one take."

This track was eventually released on the compilation album *Heaven and Hell Volume One*.

Lithium

Kurt had written all of the lyrics to "Lithium" by the time he came to Madison, though the band had yet to play the song in concert. He also knew what type of drum arrangement he wanted Chad to lay down, and he told the drummer. The bass line was, at the time, somewhat complex and busy. It would later be simplified on *Nevermind*. "I realized," says Vig, "a lot of the hooks in the songs were written by Krist on his bass. And I think Kurt basically let him come up with his own parts. They're great hooks." That observation—about the bass parts being key to many Nirvana songs—is a point not lost on other observers. "Krist is the musical anchor off of which the guitar and the vocals spring," notes Grant Alden, in 1990 the managing editor of *The Rocket*. "The drums, up until Dave Grohl, were incidental. Krist was the intuitive link. That's where the intuitive link is, between Krist and Kurt. You can add a drummer and it might make it better. But it happens between the two guys who have known each other for years, who are friends, who have been to the most rehearsals together. That's where the magic is."

Though memories of this day are hazy, observers believe this session represented a turning point in the developing rift between Cobain and Channing over Channing's drumming. Doug Olson recalls the "Lithium" session as being a "very down day" for Cobain: "Kurt was in a very sour mood. He just made everyone miserable." The problem that day seemed to stem from the fact that Chad's style and music sensibility were not meshing with Kurt's. "I remember a couple of times just sitting around with Krist and Chad," says Olson. "Chad seemed like a nice guy, but he seemed ill at ease. There was definitely something going on between him and Kurt, where Kurt was not psyched about something . . . that did come to a head at one point." Given the short window of time in which Nirvana had to record, they nevertheless stuck it out that fateful day, putting aside differences to complete an early studio recording of "Lithium."

For his part, Channing describes a relationship with Cobain where, no matter what he played at times, the band leader wasn't happy, but then again, Cobain wasn't happy with a lot of things. "It was 'The Kurt Show,'" Channing says. "He had more confidence in the live show than the records. He fell into the kind of thing where it was really hard for him to get the song idea out—sounding the way he wanted it to. Live, he felt he had more control over it. Most songs sounded the way he liked live, but the studio just didn't bring it out as much. I know Hendrix was the same way—he never liked anything that he recorded."

NIRVANA DEMOS
SMART SESSIONS

1. IN BLOOM
2. DIVE
3. LITHIUM
4. Breed
5. Boy to PLAY
6. SHAPPY
7. POLLY

Butch Vig's digital audio tape box with the songs recorded in his handwriting. Sub Pop had already taken the tape of "Here She Comes Now" before Vig had made a safety copy.

Novoselic says the major difference in "Lithium" between the Smart sessions and the Sound City sessions was that he'd improved on his bass playing during that time. "I did some work on that bass line in 'Lithium,'" he notes. "I enriched the bass playing a little more but that was about all we changed."

In comparing the Smart recording of "Lithium" to the *Nevermind* version, the arrangement is basically identical (as is true of most of the drum arrangements that Channing did during the Smart sessions on songs that were later rerecorded at Sound City). However, the nuances and the *soul* of a song can differ. Doug Olson observed, "On a song like 'Lithium,' I think the two versions are pretty similar. But you can have two different drummers play the same beat and have one guy have a great *feel* and the other guy be kind of lame. A good drummer can really make a huge difference."

Channing had grown into being an excellent drummer, but his style wasn't the sound that Cobain and Novoselic were looking for. Conflicts had increased while the band was on tour, and Kurt would literally hurl himself into Chad's drum kit at the end of a particularly tough evening. It was classic passive-aggressive behavior. But by the time of the Smart sessions, conflicts had increased to the point that Cobain wasn't being so passive anymore. At one point during the Smart sessions, Vig recalls, "Kurt climbed behind the kit and attempted to show Chad the fills on 'In Bloom.' Kurt wasn't a good drummer, but he got his ideas across." To his credit, Channing's drumming had changed over his time with Nirvana, and he'd molded his own individual playing style to fit Cobain's expectations, but that created resentment for both Channing (who hated adapting his own style) and Cobain (who still wasn't happy with the result, and who had a hard time with conflict in the first place).

Immodium

The recording of "Immodium" at Smart became a dry run for the subsequent sessions for *Nevermind* a year later. The title of the song came from a medication Kurt had observed Tad Doyle of Tad using while their bands toured together in Europe. The song would later be renamed "Breed" for *Nevermind*. Geffen's attorneys probably suggested the title change in order to avoid an intellectual property conflict with the medicine's manufacturer, McNeil Consumer Products Company. "Immodium" featured a wonderful fuzz-bass guitar riff played by Novoselic and an inventive guitar "anti-solo" by Cobain. The unorthodox solo shuns the conventional heavy-metal style of the '80s, instead relying on a rhythm-guitar form of riffing. It's a solo done with Cobain hitting all six strings at once. Vig doctored the song in the studio, moving the solo from the left to the right channel and then back again, giving the listener the impression that the guitar is three-dimensional. But the studio tinkering still didn't solve the conflict between what Cobain wanted and what he was hearing from Channing. The resulting Smart sessions version of "Immodium" was never officially released.

There were a few other fragments of songs attempted during the Smart sessions, but according to Vig and the members of Nirvana, all other songs were erased and no outtakes survive.

HERE SHE COMES NOW

While in Madison, the band decided to accept an offer to play a live show, at least partially because Vig wanted to see the band in performance. On Friday night, April 6, the band's last night in town, Nirvana headlined a sold-out concert that included Tad and a Madison band, Victim's Family. The show was at the Underground, a small bar located at the corner of Regent and Park Streets that usually attracted a college crowd. That night Nirvana packed 150 patrons into a hall with a capacity of 70.

"That was the first time I saw them live," recalls Vig. "It was a great set, very loose. I remember they were pretty messed up for it." Vig brought along Dan Hobson, the drummer from Killdozer, to see Nirvana play. Even though the band was inebriated, the show turned into a celebration of the hard work they'd accomplished in the studio during the week. After the show, Vig and Hobson stayed up all night and drank beer with Nirvana.

Also present at the Madison show was Jonathan Poneman, who had flown in to check up on the sessions and to make sure the Nirvana/Tad tour was being handled properly. Poneman had never met Vig, though the producer had done several records for Sub Pop. Though Poneman was friendly with both band and producer, he was all business when it came to the recordings. After Vig had enjoyed only an hour of sleep, Poneman woke him and sent him back into the studio. "He had to fly back fairly early the next day," says Vig. "So, he woke me up and we went into the studio early because he wanted to hear the music we'd recorded. He was real happy with it, as I recall."

Channing, however, remembers that all three members of Nirvana were disappointed that Poneman wasn't more excited about the recordings. "Usually they were more demonstrative," Channing remembers. "It was almost like we never really got a response." The drummer cites Poneman's lack of enthusiasm as one of the myriad reasons that the Smart material would never be released on Sub Pop.

Nirvana and Vig parted company the day after the Madison show, but Vig was still left working on the project. The producer had yet to mix the songs at this point, but the group had to move on for the next show of their tour. "I think I actually mixed it in about three days, tops, after they left," says Vig. The Smart Studios log notes that Vig mixed all but one song on April 11, 12, and 13. "For some reason," Vig says, "I didn't mix 'Here She Comes Now' until June 8, 1990." The producer acknowledges that the songs were not as tight and super-focused as they are on *Nevermind*, but they were looser and more raw. Reflecting back, Vig describes the Smart recordings as "definitely closer to *Bleach*."

Although the Sub Pop sessions at Smart ultimately failed to yield a second Nirvana album as planned, the recordings served as an important milestone in the band's development, if only because Cobain's songwriting had become increasingly focused and succinct. The mixture of angst-driven, piercing vocals with a pop sensibility yielded some great songs, and the band had made yet another step toward pop music, away from the raw aesthetic of *Bleach*. Though Kurt Cobain wasn't the first musician to combine noise and pop (the Velvet Underground had virtually perfected the recipe back in 1967), by the late '80s many of the post-punkers had taken the melody out of their rock. During the sessions recorded at Smart, Cobain was encouraged by Vig to put the melody back into his songs. This turning point was important not just for the songs that were done at Smart ("Lithium" sounds like it was created by an entirely different band than the Nirvana of *Bleach*), but because after this shift every song Cobain wrote in the next year (including "Come As You Are" and "Smells Like Teen Spirit") had a hook.

Novoselic and Cobain also noted later that they had felt a connection working with Vig—that he was the tangible link for them to bridge the musical gap that lay between post-punk and pop. Vig also knew enough about the alternative marketplace to make a hit song, though he'd have to wait another year to have a chance with Nirvana.

The Smart/Sub Pop recordings were initially planned for release in September 1990 as either an EP or a full-length album. Vig had thought that he might record a few more songs with the band to round out the proposed second album. But once again, fate intervened, and the old familiar "musical differences" and record-label concerns scrambled the picture for Nirvana.

The biggest problem became the perennial drummer conflict. The band finished up their tour of the western United States, but tensions continued between Chad and Krist and Kurt. "Chad wanted to express himself in a way that really didn't jell with the band," Novoselic explained diplomatically in an interview in 1991. Today he echoes that sentiment: "Chad was more of a softer-style drummer, but he changed to be harder and more rhythmic. He didn't like doing that," Novoselic says.

According to Channing, he wasn't happy either, though he felt that a lot of the tension in the band came from the high workload Cobain put on himself. When Channing offered to help write songs, Cobain encouraged him, though he never used his material, and ultimately Channing felt resentful.

After the tour ground to a halt in late May, tensions between Channing and Cobain came to a head. Though just one year earlier Cobain had been telling journalists that Channing was the greatest drummer around, by May 1990, he was criticizing everything about Channing's style, and, perhaps unfairly, claiming that the drummer couldn't keep time. He told Michael Azerrad, "[Chad] really had bad timing and he wasn't a very powerful drummer." Cobain's version of the story of Channing's departure would change over the years. However, in early 1992 he told Paddy Chng, "Chad just wanted to leave, although I'm not sure why."

There were some observers, though, who felt that Channing had improved and was a reasonable fit for Nirvana. Jack Endino, for one, defends Channing's drumming, saying, "I can't speculate on why they fired Chad, but I think it was personal, that they didn't get along. Because I think his drumming had come along quite a ways by the time they got rid of him. He had a style he was adding. He was getting there."

Channing himself confirms that the reason for the final blowup was growing differences in style, perhaps best described as "creative differences." Though that particular excuse has routinely been cited by numerous bands for conflicts that in actuality were outside of the musical arena, in the case of Channing and Cobain, it was accurate. The two men liked and respected each other but simply had different ideas about the style of drumming the band needed. "I began to feel like a drum machine," Channing recalls. "I was losing interest, and it was totally showing, just in my lack of interest in playing a lot of shows. Kurt and Krist realized it. It should have come up a lot earlier, and I should have brought it up. I made the situation be one where they had to come up to me and say, 'This isn't working out.'" Cobain and Novoselic drove out to his house on Bainbridge Island and told him the news.

Seattle photographer Charles Peterson believes that Chad's departure was foretold by a photo session the band did that spring at his studio. "I just had a piece of white seamless paper hung up," he said in *Teen Spirit: The Kurt Cobain Tribute Video*. "And Kurt comes in and he says, 'I just hate white seamless paper. It has nothing to do with punk rock or us or anything.' So I said, 'Well, here's a can of spray paint, do something. I don't know what else to do with you guys.' So he painted a plus and a minus, without hesitating, on the piece of paper. It was perfect. It definitely had connotations because the way most of the shots were done,

Chad was sitting under the minus sign. And I think about two weeks later, he was out of the band."

Once Chad had departed, the two original band members decided not to release the Smart sessions in an album format. Novoselic explains: "We knew [the Smart session] wasn't going to be our next record at that point."

The band enlisted Mudhoney's drummer, Dan Peters, to record a quick single for Sub Pop called "Sliver." Sub Pop rushed it out and used "Dive" from the Smart sessions as the B-side. At the same time, Sub Pop began holding conversations with major labels about the prospect of licensing and distributing its stable of artists. Sub Pop's actions did not sit well with the band and led to a growing rift between Nirvana and the label.

At this point, Novoselic says, Nirvana decided their days on Sub Pop were numbered. "We knew we wanted to sign with a major label," he says. "We felt that everyone else—Dinosaur Jr. and Sonic Youth—had all signed to majors and we thought that was a good way to get some cash. And Sub Pop was always on the brink of bankruptcy. Always."

Cobain was dissatisfied with Sub Pop over their promotion of *Bleach*. He was constantly asking for the band's royalty statements. Though these particular complaints are common ones from bands on independent labels, they were far too common in the case of the bands on Sub Pop. The biggest issue may have been distribution: Cobain and Novoselic frequently complained to journalists that their Sub Pop releases couldn't be found in record stores they visited while touring.

While Nirvana continued to tour and develop their own grassroots underground buzz, the Smart session tapes began to circulate within the music industry. Unbeknownst to Sub Pop, Nirvana began to hawk the Smart sessions to outside major labels and distribute copies to important people in the industry and to other bands. Doug Olson recalls, "After Butch had recorded the Sub Pop Nirvana sessions, it seemed like every band that came into Smart had a copy of the tape. Oftentimes it was a really crappy fourth-generation, horrible cassette dub. [But] every band that would come in was really into it."

Meanwhile, in Seattle, the tape became the one cassette that everyone in the city had to get a dub of. "They had actually made up these demo tapes," recalls Endino. "They gave me the tape and it said 'Nirvana' on it with this little hand-made cover. There were six or seven songs, plus

Nirvana playing one of their most important shows ever at the Motor Sports Garage, September 22, 1990. Notice Dan Peters, of Mudhoney, on drums. (Photograph by Alice Wheeler)

they had put 'Love Buzz' on the end of it. And they were calling it a demo. In other words, they were shopping it. And Krist said, 'Don't tell Sub Pop I gave this to you, but this is what we're sending out to try to get a deal.' They were giving it out trying to get some interest."

Novoselic now looks back on the summer of 1990 as one of the low points in the band's history. For all practical purposes, Nirvana didn't exist, as they could neither play live nor record. Cobain and Novoselic soon focused on the two things they desperately needed to become a band again: "We went looking," Novoselic remembers, "for another drummer and for a deal."

SMELLS LIKE TEEN SPIRIT

On a hot Friday night almost six months after the Smart sessions ended, Kurt Cobain and Krist Novoselic drove home from Sea-Tac airport with their new drummer sitting in the backseat of the van. It was September 21, 1990, and during the one-hour ride from the airport to Cobain's home in Olympia, Dave Grohl got to know his new bandmates. He offered Cobain a bite of an apple and, according to Cobain biographer Michael Azerrad, Kurt said, "No thanks, it'll make my teeth bleed." In a fictional account of his first meeting with the band for the official DGC "biography" of Nirvana, Grohl provided a satirical explanation of his initial impressions of Kurt and Krist: "They wore berets, sunglasses, sandals and had goatees. Krist walked around with these poetry books by Rod McKuen, and Kurt would do interpretive dances while Krist recited Rod McKuen's poetry."

During the summer of 1990, when not reciting bad poetry, Cobain and Novoselic had continued their search for a permanent drummer. From time to time, they borrowed Dale Crover from the Melvins, and they enlisted the talents of Mudhoney drummer Dan Peters for one infamous show at Seattle's Motor Sports Garage. But these stopgap measures were not the answer; once again, the almost divine intervention of Melvins singer Buzz Osborne came into play. Osborne suggested a drummer who would complete the trio that would make for the most well-known lineup of Nirvana, and the one that would find the most success.

Dave Grohl was born in 1969 in Warren, Ohio, and like his future bandmates, he was the product of a broken home. In the autumn of 1990, he was also the victim of a broken band, as his group Scream had

disintegrated while on tour. Growing up, Grohl had played in several D.C.-area garage bands, including Freak Baby, Mission Impossible, and his earliest high-school band, of which he told *The Rocket* in 1996, "I think we might have been called 'Nameless.' Really!"

Grohl wasn't nameless for long. With Scream he'd developed a reputation within indie rock circles, and Novoselic and Cobain had caught the band's San Francisco show and had been impressed. Though Scream had been slowly gaining a larger following, in the summer of 1990 they broke up in Los Angeles after their bass player quit the band. It left Grohl broke and about as far away from D.C. as one could get in the U.S. "We got stranded," Grohl remembered on *Nevermind: It's an Interview.* "There wasn't really much to do. I called my friend Buzz Osborne, who is a singer for the Melvins. We'd known each other for a while. And he ended up introducing me to [Nirvana]." In a 1992 interview, Novoselic recounted seeing Dave play with Scream: "We were just blown away by the whole band. Especially the drummer. Their drummer was really good. When he called, we said, 'Yeah, man, come on up.'"

Though Grohl had to put up with the eccentricities of his new bandmates (including having to live with Cobain in his self-described "hellhole" apartment in Olympia), the musical connection between the three musicians was almost immediate, according to all concerned. "Everyone loves him, and he plays drums better than any drummer I've ever heard," Cobain enthused on *Nevermind: It's an Interview.* Cobain even compared Grohl to legendary Led Zeppelin drummer John Bonham: "He blows away Bonham, and if I had a choice of bringing John Bonham back to life or [choosing] any drummer of any band I could even think of, they wouldn't be better than Dave. He's great."

The addition of Grohl was pivotal in Nirvana's music's assuming a degree of maturity. Compared to the previous drummers the band had worked with, Grohl had two obvious strengths: he could play hard, and he was able to combine that power with subtlety when required. A 1991 profile in *The Rocket* described Grohl's approach to drumming: "He wails on them like he has a personal vendetta and wants those drums dead." In many ways, Cobain wasn't far off in comparing Grohl to Zeppelin's Bonham because, like Bonham and Keith Moon, Grohl pounded the drums so hard that they took on their own explosive power, and because of his prowess he drew musicians to Nirvana's shows just to watch him

At the Motor Sports Garage show. Dave Grohl had arrived in Seattle the day before only to watch the band play with Dan Peters this night.
(Photograph by Alice Wheeler)

Kurt Cobain playing horizontally at the Motor Sports Garage show.
(PHOTOGRAPH BY ALICE WHEELER)

play. Grohl's style coalesced with Nirvana's bass-driven songs and turned them into dangerous, focused, aggressive anthems. After settling on Grohl as their drummer, Cobain called up Butch Vig to express his excitement. "He shouted over the phone that he had found the loudest drummer in the world," Vig remembers. Cobain told Vig of Grohl: "He is so amazing and so solid and so loud that we can play how we *need* to play as a band now."

Major labels had been interested in Nirvana as far back as *Bleach*, but at that point the band members weren't interested in switching to the majors. Years of frustration with Sub Pop had changed their attitude. "The accounting was screwed up, and we didn't get paid for a long time," Cobain told *Big O* magazine's Paddy Chng in 1992. "The distribution was inadequate too. We had kids coming up to us saying they couldn't find our records anywhere. That's when we decided that we should leave Sub Pop."

While the band toured Europe that fall and continued rehearsing (and even found time for a short recording session in January at Seattle's The Music Source that would yield the eventual B-side "Aneurysm"), every major label except Warner Bros. made offers or entered into negotiations with the band.

Perhaps the height of the A&R frenzy came on November 25, 1990, when Nirvana played a show at Seattle's tiny club Off Ramp. "The A&R guys were in full court press," remembers Damon Stewart, a local DJ who had just begun working for Sony, and who was also a friend of the band. At least six different A&R reps from the likes of Slash, Columbia, Charisma, and MCA attended this one show.

The band played the bidding war for all the free dinners they could, getting their first taste of major-label largesse. "We felt like snotty little hot-shot kids," Grohl later told Michael Azerrad. "We felt like we were getting away with something." Grohl soon figured out that most of the A&R executives that were wooing the band had previously worked at Tower Records, his former employer. "They were wining and dining us," said Novoselic on *Nevermind: It's an Interview*.

The band employed a lawyer named Alan Mintz to shop around their Smart demos, and he was the point man for negotiations. Nirvana weighed factors in considering the various labels, choosing not to go with some of the more corporate labels, though they still took advantage of any free-dinner offer. "It was the ultimate bidding war," remembers Lisa Fancher of Frontier Records. "You had some people boasting that they'd actually signed the band to their labels, only to have the group then announce that Geffen was their choice."

In November 1990, they finally settled on their choice of label, and Mintz called up the A&R rep who had won: Jeff Fenster of Charisma, a new U.S. rock label distributed by Virgin. "He called me up and said, 'Jeff, congratulations, Nirvana are signing with Charisma Records.'" To Fenster, the band's decision was the culmination of two years of wooing them. In the previous year alone he'd seen dozens of shows and followed them on the road, befriending the group in the process. But Fenster was experienced enough to know that no deal is done until it is signed. He had his office send a letter finalizing the deal out to Mintz the next day. And then he waited, but neither the band nor Mintz returned his calls.

Charisma wasn't the only label thinking they had signed Nirvana, though they probably were the only one that had direct communication from the band saying they were onboard. Several other major labels also thought they had the band in their camp, based on things said by the group, and by the way their negotiations had gone.

Then something changed as Nirvana began to shop for management during the same week they were negotiating their record deal. The band made a decision to sign with Gold Mountain Management, a firm run by John Silva and Danny Goldberg, and their new managers stepped in at the eleventh hour and arranged a deal with Geffen Records, on the DGC imprint (DGC stands for David Geffen Company). Two things helped Geffen win the band away from other bidders: Gold Mountain had a close relationship with the label, and Sonic Youth were on Geffen. On April 30, 1991, the official agreement for the band to record on the DGC label was signed, and Fenster and the other labels were out of luck. There would be no looking back for the onetime indie band. Though the decision to sign with a major label was a huge one for the band, it mirrored a similar journey taken by other former indie bands R.E.M., Hüsker Dü, and the Replacements, all bands that Nirvana admired.

When asked by *Hype* magazine six days before the release of *Nevermind* why they had signed with Geffen, Cobain and Novoselic played their typical Laurel and Hardy roles and confirmed yet again that it was the Sonic Youth card that drew them in to this particular major label. Kurt: "[At Geffen] it didn't seem like anyone cared or knew about us, that's what appealed to us." Novoselic: "But there were some people there that had worked at, like, [the labels] Rough Trade and SST." Kurt: "Who generally seemed to know about underground music." Novoselic: "And Sonic Youth is there too, and that's cool."

Instead of signing for the rumored "big bonus," the band wisely chose to negotiate for a stronger contract that would give them greater artistic independence and a larger royalty percentage. It was a gamble that would have left the band in debt if *Nevermind* hadn't been successful. Geffen also had to buy out Sub Pop, and the indie label received a nominal seventy-five thousand dollars plus a share of future album royalties. Kurt was quick to defend Nirvana's major-label jump to the media and fans alike. "We haven't compromised," he told a radio station reporter in 1992. "Our record label lets us do anything we want. People calling us sellouts forget that groups like the Ramones and the Sex Pistols were on major labels." Cobain was partially incorrect: the Sex Pistols were actually on Virgin in the U.K., an indie label, and the Ramones were on Sire in the U.S., a quasi indie within the larger Warner Bros. corporation.

The band began rehearsing for *Nevermind* in early 1991. They rented a barnlike structure that was located in the backyard of a friend's house in Tacoma. On *Nevermind: It's an Interview*, Grohl described the friend's facility as "This *thing* that had a studio in it. Upstairs, his brother lived, and he was in this really bad Howard Johnson lounge band. Everything was carpeted with this brown shag carpet. He even had stage lights in there and a massive PA that he just did not know how to use." After writing and forgetting many new songs, the band bought a boom box to capture their working demos. "We came up with so much stuff where we'd go, 'God, this is the best thing we've ever done!'" Grohl told *Circus*. "Then we'd forget how to play it. So many songs got thrown away, until we finally said, 'Maybe we should start recording them on a cassette.' So we'd record them, then lose the cassette." One of the cassettes that was not lost was labeled "Smells Like Teen Spirit."

In the early spring of 1991, Nirvana and DGC began to search for a producer to record Nirvana's major-label debut. R.E.M. producer Scott Litt was considered early on, as was another famous Southerner, Don Dixon. The band also considered Neil Young producer David Briggs, and both Briggs and Dixon were flown to the Northwest to meet with the band in their Tacoma barn. "Gary Gersh [Nirvana's Geffen A&R rep] brought up David Briggs, rest his soul," Novoselic says of the now deceased Briggs. "We played a few songs for David, and he was into it. And then we went out to Denny's and had coffee and we just wanted to hear all these Neil Young stories. Then the same day, Gersh also brought Don Dixon and we hung out with him a bit."

At one point, according to Butch Vig, there was a plan for Dixon to produce while Vig engineered. "I thought that would have been a cool idea," says Vig. "My group, Fire Town, had actually wanted to work with him to produce the Fire Town record. And I liked his work with the Smithereens." But the idea of a Dixon/Vig production team was quickly abandoned, most likely, Vig recalls, because of scheduling conflicts and budget constraints. Cobain told one fanzine in early 1991 that Vig would most likely produce, but that other producers might also be used on the project for the songs that were "commercial."

While Nirvana was rehearsing in their barnyard building, Vig was back home in Madison producing the album *Gish* for a then-obscure band called Smashing Pumpkins. He had heard about Nirvana's signing with Geffen and was pleased with their rapid rise from an underground indie band to major-label players. Though he had worked well with Nirvana a year earlier, Vig had his doubts that executives at Geffen would allow Nirvana to choose an unknown indie knob-twiddler to produce their big-league debut.

Vig relates what happened next: "It wasn't that they [Geffen] didn't want me to do it. I think they just thought it would be good to put Nirvana in with someone more experienced. Because really, they didn't know who I was. I was still working on an independent level. I had done those [Nirvana] demos that were actually supposed to be a Sub Pop record. Anyway, at the eleventh hour, I was doing *Gish*. Billy [Corgan] kept saying, 'Are you going to do the new Nirvana?' I said, 'I don't know, I have no idea. No one's called.' And then all of a sudden Geffen and their management called and said, 'Can you get out here in a week or two and do this record?' I said, 'Sure.'"

Aware that Nirvana had talked to other producers first, Butch believes "the band kind of held out for me, because I think I still had a sensibility for where they were coming from. From more of the punk ethic. And they were afraid of going with someone who might make them too slick or just not understand what they were about."

Novoselic confirms this, saying that the band felt comfortable with Vig and pushed for him to be the choice. "We'd worked with him before and he was so encouraging," Krist says. "He drove the band, but in a positive way. We were nervous already about being on a major label, and then it was like, we were going to have these mainstream producers? We asked for Don Dixon because he was really good, and we asked for David Briggs because he was good. They were some of the choices we were presented with [from the label]. We chose from that list and said, 'These guys are cool.' But when it came down to the wire, we just sort of chickened out. We really liked Butch because we were really comfortable working with him." Novoselic says that the band had to feverishly lobby Geffen to get them to agree on the selection of Vig. "The label likes to go for a safe bet and they said, 'Who is this guy who does Killdozer records and stuff?' But we said, 'We want Butch,' and they eventually said okay."

After agreeing to produce *Nevermind*, Vig did have a few nervous moments before heading out to California. "I was very freaked out about it," he recalls. "I was thinking that I'm going to a studio I've never been in before, I have a bigger budget here, and I'm doing it for a major label. It was *very* intimidating."

In the days before he packed up to leave for Los Angeles, Vig received an enthusiastic phone call from Kurt. "He seemed to be really excited about playing again." Cobain told Vig he would be sending some tapes of songs the band had recently recorded on a cheap boom box, and he raved to the producer about Dave Grohl. Vig says he thought to himself, "'Yeah, right, I've heard that one before.' But it turned out to be true!" From his earlier work with the band at Smart, Butch was familiar with several of the distorted boom-box songs Kurt sent to him. But Vig heard new songs as well, and he could tell the band had grown stronger thanks to the extra dimension added by Dave's drumming. The presence of Grohl had turned the band into a much tighter and more powerful trio. "The other thing I noticed," says Butch, "was that the new songs were much better crafted and hook-y."

MEXICAN SEAFOOD

In the last week of April 1991, Novoselic drove his Volkswagen van to Los Angeles while Cobain and Grohl followed in the band's trusty Dodge van. When they arrived in Los Angeles, the first place they headed was Universal Studios.

Not far away was their second stop: Sound City Recording Studios in Van Nuys. "It was built back in 1964," says studio manager Shivaun O'Brien. "Back then, it was called Vox Studios." Later renamed Sound City, the secluded recording facility has over the years played host to a number of fabled rock 'n' roll musicians, and the building's résumé lists over fifty gold and platinum record awards in three decades, though it is the studio's Vox amps that most clients still remember.

When they described the studio for *Nevermind: It's an Interview*, each member of the band had a different impression of Sound City. Kurt said, "The board and the room are really old." To Dave it was "like, pretty techno." Novoselic was most impressed by the studio's history: "All the dinosaurs recorded there, like Fleetwood Mac and Cheap Trick."

It was the studio's pedigree that attracted the band—the most important albums recorded there were Tom Petty's *Damn the Torpedoes* and parts of Fleetwood Mac's *Rumours*, though Nirvana were also impressed by being at the birthplace of Cheap Trick's *Heaven Tonight* and Foreigner's *Double Vision*. But truth be told, by 1991 Sound City was on its last legs. "It was really in a state of disarray," says O'Brien. "It was ready to be closed. This was an era when everything in Los Angeles was going digital."

The outside of Sound City
Recording Studios where
Nirvana recorded
Nevermind.
(PHOTOGRAPH BY LOREN
ALBERT)

Sound City didn't even have a very convenient location. Van Nuys, California, is a suburban community located in the San Fernando Valley, sixteen miles northwest of downtown Los Angeles, a journey that could take an hour with traffic. The studio is located in an industrial park, in a neighborhood famous as the headquarters of some of the larger pornographic film companies. Surrounding the studio are car dealerships, a Holiday Inn frequented by long-haul truckers, and personal storage facilities. Though the neighborhood isn't glamorous, the studio's location is advantageous in that it is a discreet place, a secluded location to work in away from the spotlight. The only indication that one has arrived at the studio is a floor mat at the front door that reads "Sound City." The entrance door has a foreboding sign, warning off fans and reporters, that admission is for "Clients & Personnel Only."

Not that many fans would have been looking for the place in 1991. The clients in the studio before Nirvana, who actually did some mixing work in the smaller studio while *Nevermind* was being recorded, were the metal band Warrant, who had already reached their career peak. "Mostly, in those days, we attracted big-hair bands here," says O'Brien. "Big rooms like this were dying because everyone wanted digital, and they wanted specialized studios." What Sound City did offer was a huge room (the main studio is forty by fifty feet, with a twenty-five-foot-high ceiling) and a "big sound." It couldn't have been more perfect for *Nevermind*. It was also cheap, which was one of the main reasons the label and management had suggested it: Nirvana was charged five hundred dollars a day. By comparison, at the time many of the larger studios in Los Angeles were charging three or four times that amount.

During their six-week residency in California, the band stayed in a Van Nuys apartment complex close to the studio. The short-term lease was arranged by Nirvana's Gold Mountain management company, and the owners of the building regretted it almost from the instant the band moved in. It did not take long for the apartment to take on the appearance of a scene from the film *Animal House* as the band lived the punk lifestyle together. Vig—who was staying at a budget motel not far away—recalls visiting Nirvana's home quarters during the recording sessions: "It was chaos. There was graffiti on the walls, and the couches were upside-down. They would stay up every night and go down to Venice Beach until six o'clock in the morning."

Before they began working at Sound City, the band spent a few days at yet another rehearsal space rented for them in North Hollywood. Vig visited them several times but decided not to force them to practice the songs too much, "Because I didn't want them to burn out on the songs before we went in to record them." Then, on May 2, 1991, the band and Vig settled into Sound City for sessions that originally were booked for less than three weeks. Vig says his strategy going in was to keep the sessions "au naturel" to reflect the live feel of the band. The band planned to re-record some of the Smart Studios tracks and tackle a few newly written compositions.

Though the band was well rehearsed, having spent considerable time in Tacoma jamming and a lesser but more focused period of time in Los Angeles preparing, much of the material was still new to them. Of the thirteen tracks that were released on *Nevermind*, six of the songs had never been performed live before. Two of the songs that had been played live, "Territorial Pissings" and "Smells Like Teen Spirit," had been performed only at one concert. And even the Smart songs were new to Grohl, who, at the time the Sound City sessions began, had been playing with the band for just a little over seven months.

One can only imagine what Kurt Cobain must have thought entering Sound City that May afternoon; compared to the previous studios the group had worked in—Smart and Reciprocal—the place was gigantic. In fact, studio A of Sound City was bigger than Smart and Reciprocal put together. Their new home also boasted something not found at either of their old locales: as you entered the facility, the halls were lined with gold and platinum record awards. Seeing a gold record for the Rick Springfield album *Living in Oz*, one can only wonder if Cobain thought he was living in an alternate universe.

Those gold albums impressed Novoselic, who also noticed the awards for records by Evil Knievel, Dio, and Ratt. "We realized it wasn't some big Hollywood, hoity-toity place," Novoselic recalls. "And we always liked working on Neve boards and we saw that it had a Neve board."

The band did find something familiar, though: ugly brown carpeting, not unlike that which had covered their barnyard rehearsal space. The lounge area also featured ugly brown sofas and snack and pop machines, and the ubiquitous video game in the hall. It wasn't fancy, but, as O'Brien says, "Smoking was definitely allowed," an important factor for Grohl and Cobain, who were nicotine addicts. The studio also allowed its clients to burn whatever they wished inside the rooms. For Nirvana's sessions, according to O'Brien, there were candles everywhere.

Three of the four walls in studio A were painted stark white with large, colorful murals of the Los Angeles skyline as decoration. The fourth featured wood paneling from floor to ceiling with tri-pane window cutouts looking into the control room. Adjustable track lighting offered the band a range of atmospheres, from the stark brightness of morning to the romantic twilight of an evening sunset. The ceiling was lined with dozens of white rectangular sound baffles. Before Nirvana began recording, the scene looked like an army preparing for musical Armageddon: miles of cords, jacks, multiple amps, guitar cases, effects pedals, Grohl's drum kit, and an endless supply of mikes and stands began to fill up the busy room. In one corner near the control window stood a black piano, brought in for this session, ready and waiting if needed. It would collect dust.

A door from the studio led into the darkened control room, which would serve as Vig's musical command post for the next month and a

Sound City's Studio A where the band did most of their recording.
(PHOTOGRAPH BY LOREN ALBERT)

half. Four playback monitors rested on top of the control board's late-model, wood-grained Neve console. From the center of the board, Vig's point of view looked straight out at Grohl's kit. A clock on the wall behind the drum kit marked the minutes and hours as Nirvana progressed from underground band to international sensation.

Vig explains the general recording setup: "I recorded them basically live in the studio. We set up drum mikes, and I put a drum tunnel on the bass drum and wired up the kit with standard mikes. Then I placed some [Neuman] U87s about twenty feet from the drums to try and pump up the room sound.

"We went through the Neve board," Vig continues. "Krist Novoselic used an SVT bass rig. Kurt Cobain, for the most part, used a Mesa Boogie amp. We also had him use a Fender Bassman." Butch's job description required him to engineer the album as well. Tuning Dave's drums, positioning mikes, checking sound levels, and schlepping gear back and forth were all part and parcel of the engineer's job. Jeff Sheehan, Sound City's in-house engineer, pitched in to familiarize the producer with available

NEVERMIND/NIRVANA

studio resources. Vig did get some help with the drums from Ross Garfield, known to the music industry as the "Drum Doctor," who helped Vig tune the drums on several visits to the studio.

Garfield describes the sessions as "relaxed." There were no early indications that this particular album had the potential to stand out from any other being made at the time. "I got the vibe that nobody in the room expected the album to do what it did," he remembers. Garfield recalls Novoselic as very outgoing, friendly, and jovial at the sessions. "Having a name like Drum Doctor invites jokes," he says, and the bass player offered up more than a few. As for Cobain, Garfield recalls him as "just kind of brooding on the couch. Kurt seemed to just sit back and sort of question things."

Vig's plan was to record the band live, doubletrack some rhythm guitars, and then overdub some additional guitar riffs and other subtle accents. His was a vérité approach to recording. Vig explains: "They sounded so amazing live that in order to get that kind of sound on record you had to use more production work in the studio: doubling guitars, using multiple mikes on things and splitting them left and right, just trying to make it sound larger than life."

As with all Nirvana recording sessions, getting a good drum sound was the most important goal. Prior to the sessions, Vig had called in Garfield to provide a Tama Artstar II set of drums with a sixteen-by-twenty-four-inch bass drum; a twelve-by-fifteen-inch rack tom; and a sixteen-by-eighteen-inch floor tom. The drums were provided to Grohl as part of an endorsement deal, courtesy of Tama and the Drum Doctor. However, the single most influential piece of gear Vig reserved was "the Terminator." "That's the one piece that really stands out when you listen to the album," recalls Garfield. "It's a six-and-a-half-inch-by-fourteen-inch bell brass Black Beauty drum that weighs a lot, at least five times heavier than any other snare drum I've got." The need for the

A receipt for $1500 worth of drums Nirvana rented for the Sound City sessions—cheap at any price.

Terminator was directly related to the band's express desire to achieve a heavy sound in their music. "It had an amazing sound," says Vig. "We used it on every track except 'Polly' and 'Something in the Way.'" It created a sound that Garfield describes as having "a lot of low-end as well as crack to it, so you get that real nice punchy, rock 'n' roll sound."

Novoselic brought the least amount of equipment, with the most important pieces of gear being his two Gibson Ripper bass guitars and an Ampeg SVT 400 bass amp. He also had Peavey and Fender two-by-fifteen bass amps. By comparison, Cobain brought to the session a small arsenal of guitars to propel his electric aggression. He carried in a late-'60s Mustang, a Jaguar with DiMarzio pickups, an old Stella acoustic, a rare left-handed Mosrite, and some new Stratocasters. The band was poised to rock.

THE SONGS:
SOUND CITY SESSIONS

Kurt Cobain's ability to write songs with such strong hooks was the crucial ingredient to Nirvana's eventual worldwide appeal. The melodies he wrote were so memorable, people found themselves singing along without even knowing or understanding the lyrics. Dave Grohl tried his hand at describing the song structures on *Nevermind* when he told a British television show, "It's the kind of stuff that sticks in your head. Because the songs are so simple, basic and stark. Just like the children's songs you hear as a kid. You know, you remember those your whole life." The early influence of Lennon and McCartney served Cobain well. "Kurt loved the Beatles," recalls Vig. "He loved John Lennon. So I know that he felt self-conscious, coming from a punk background and having these kind of gorgeously crafted rock songs. Even though his songs might have been kind of noisy, they still had really beautiful melodies and melodic structure." And like the Beatles' best work, the songs written for *Nevermind* were simple and catchy, yet elegant.

The Beatles' influence contrasted with the years Cobain spent listening to Black Sabbath, Kiss, and Led Zeppelin. As a budding guitarist, Cobain often lowered the tuning of his guitar strings to accentuate the heavy sound he was searching for. Cobain's subsequent immersion in punk music attracted him to angular, jagged chord changes: sudden lurches that created a type of discomfort became his trademark. Thus, the songs of *Nevermind* were a blending of musical genres that had not been attempted before, and there was a sense of musical schizophrenia about them. Repetitive pop melodies would lull listeners into a relaxed groove, only to have a raging, wailing chorus barge in, powered by the hostility and tension in Kurt's shredding vocal cords.

"Kurt's whole songwriting was about melody," Novoselic says. "He had a knack for it. The vocal would play off the guitar and hook you in. I played off the vocals and the drums. We weren't some art project or some statement."

Lyrically, Cobain's compositions were a jumble of ideas, and within any one song there might be several different viewpoints. Rarely did one song contain a single theme. As Cobain explained it to a British television interviewer, "Most of the lyrics are just like contradictions. I'll write a few sincere lines and then I'll have to make fun of it with another line. I don't like to make things too obvious. Because if it is too obvious, it gets really stale. We don't mean to be really cryptic or mysterious. But I just think that lyrics that are different and kind of weird paint a nice picture. It's just the way I like art."

The first problem facing Cobain was that when the band went into the studio not all his lyrics were finished. "Some of the songs weren't written until just before we recorded the album," Cobain would later tell *The Rocket*. "And most of the lyrics were written while we were recording. In fact, on a couple of days everyone had to wait around for me to finish the lyrics." Novoselic echoed this sentiment to *The Rocket*: "We were just standing there with our arms crossed and our feet tapping, just staring at Kurt as he sat there sweating and writing and looking and writing and looking. Just breathing down his throat, so that pressure element was there. I think the pressure element was healthy."

Smells Like Teen Spirit

The lead-off song on any album holds an important position because, in many cases, it is the first aural contact the listener has with a band. For a fickle record-buying public, first impressions are crucial. When the band set up to record this track, there was no sense that the song would turn into a multimedia monster or that the media would ultimately dub it "the anthem of Generation X."

"Smells Like Teen Spirit" had its genesis one night as Kurt was drinking beer with his friend Kathleen Hanna (of the band Bikini Kill) at

his Olympia home. "My friend and I were in my bedroom drunk," Kurt told Patrick MacDonald of the *Seattle Times* in an interview on the day of *Nevermind's* release. "We were having a really fun time talking about all kinds of revolutionary things, and we ended up destroying my bedroom. We ended up throwing my art supplies all over, and paint, and breaking the mirror, and tearing my bed up. It was a lot of fun. And so we were writing all over the wall with paint and my friend wrote, 'Kurt smells like teen spirit,' and I took that as a compliment. What she actually meant by it was that I smelled like this deodorant that is for teenagers called Teen Spirit. She'd seen it on television and I guess I stunk that night."

As to the larger theme of the song, Cobain told MacDonald, "It's basically just about friends. The friends that we have now, in a way. We still feel as if we're teenagers because we don't follow the guidelines of what's expected of us to be adults. We still screw around and have a good time. It also has kind of a teen revolutionary theme to it." As Cobain did more and more interviews while the album and song took off, his story

The view from Sound City's Studio A toward the control room.
(Photograph by Loren Albert)

began to change and he was rarely specific about what "Teen Spirit" meant, if he answered that question at all.

The liner notes to *Nevermind* state that all of the album's lyrics are written by Kurt Cobain. However, the certificate of registration for "Smells Like Teen Spirit," filed with the United States Copyright Office on October 8, 1991, credits the song's "words and music as contained on *Nevermind*" to all three band members. Virgin Songs, Inc., is listed as the author of the work, as employer for Cobain, Novoselic and Grohl, "by virtue of written agreement." The 1993 publication of transcribed guitar music for *Nevermind,* released by the Hal Leonard Corporation, also credits this recording to all three members of the band; it is the only song on the record so credited.

Novoselic remembers vividly the first time Cobain brought the song in to practice: "Kurt was playing just the chorus, 'When the light's out, and it's dangerous, here we are now,' over and over again. I said, 'Wait a minute, why don't we just kind of slow this down a bit?' So I just started playing the verse part. And Dave starting doing this drum beat. And that's a whole different part of the song. It's not like we wrote the whole song— we just sort of turned it around a bit."

A rough recording of an early "Teen Spirit" was one of the distorted boom-box cassettes Cobain had sent to Butch before the sessions began. Vig instantly liked the song: "Kurt sent me a tape of them recorded in the basement on a boom box. Terrible recording. I couldn't hear any vocals, but I heard the opening guitar riffs. And then it just kicks in—total boom-box distortion!" Vig admits that because of the poor quality of the tape he could not hear Kurt singing, "Except I could kind of hear the part, 'Hello, hello' with the riff." Vig says he played the tape for his wife, and her reaction was, "What is this? This sounds terrible." But Vig was sold on the song from the power of the distorted tape. "[I kept thinking], 'Man, I don't know, this sounds awesome.' You could tell with the chord progression. It just sounds really powerful."

Vig first heard the band play the song one week before the Sound City sessions began, at the Los Angeles rehearsal space. "The first time they played it, it stunned me," he recalls enthusiastically. "The rehearsal space was one of these rooms that is very loud to begin with. The sound pressure builds up. And they were playing at stun volume, and it just floored me! I knew it was a really great song." It was one of the few songs during that rehearsal time that Vig deliberately made the band play over and over, simply because, he says, "I was really into it."

When it came time to record "Teen Spirit" at Sound City, Vig suggested a few changes to the arrangement. He moved the guitar/vocal ad-lib from the outro to a point after each chorus. Then he cut the solo down from its original concert length. "I think we changed the chorus to six progressions instead of eight," says Butch. "I wanted the song to keep building to this explosive release. It was pretty subtle arranging that I did. I just paced around the room thinking, 'This is just an incredibly powerful song.' Very cathartic." Kurt used an Electro-Harmonix Small Clone as one of the effects on the prechorus buildup to "Teen Spirit." The Small Clone was the key to the chiming guitar sound heard on the song.

Putting together "Smells Like Teen Spirit" was like baking a multi-layered wedding cake: following standard recording techniques, Vig constructed the foundation (the bass and drums) first and then built layers and layers on top of it. He first recorded Grohl's drum part and Novoselic's bass, utilizing the first ten of twenty-four available tracks. Tracks 11 and 12 were reserved to record the basic live band performance. "Then I'd go back and punch in corrections and tighten up the performance," he says, "because Kurt was having difficulties getting the timing right on the effects pedals for switching between different sounds." For the guitar part, Cobain chose the Fender Bassman amp. Take 1 of only two total takes was deemed the best. However, upon repeated listening, Vig decided to use both takes in the mix. He doubletracked the twin guitar parts and used them in tandem, panning left and right. "Kurt did two passes on it, though he didn't really want to," says Vig. "But he was great at playing because he had his parts figured out very well."

Vig was only able to coax three vocal takes out of Kurt on "Teen Spirit." "I was lucky to ever get Kurt to do four takes," recalls Vig. "Usually, he would only do two or three." The best parts of all three takes were combined to create a composite vocal master which was then placed on to track 15. Vig then asked Kurt to isolate his vocal part, "hello, hello, hello, how low," for dropping in. This allowed Kurt to get tight on the mike and perfect the phrasing. The overdubbed "hello" bridge was placed onto tracks 21 and 22. Having finished the main vocal parts, Kurt then dou-

Sound City's control room looking out toward Studio A. (Photograph by Loren Albert)

bletracked the chorus vocals as well. The last step for producer Vig was to select track 20's chorus as the "hot" one and move it down to track 15 with the master vocal take. In a fairly short time, "Smells Like Teen Spirit" was assembled and in the can. It was one of the easiest recordings during the Sound City sessions.

Even before the song was completely finished, the band and the producer were aware that it was a powerful performance. "I remember listening to 'Teen Spirit' after Kurt did the vocals," Novoselic says. "I said to myself, 'Whoa, this is really raw.' There was a lot of energy there."

"Smells Like Teen Spirit" at once mocks the concept of youth rebellion and musically embraces it. Cobain's rebel ambivalence mirrors a young John Lennon, who could not decide whether the listener should count him "in/out" on the Beatles song "Revolution." If nothing else, "Teen Spirit" seemed to embody the helplessness and apathy of a generation. However, the song may well have been a personal look into Kurt's own life rather than a rebel call to arms for his disaffected generation. In digging deep into the song's third verse, one finds the source of the album's title and theme. Cobain sings about how he's forgotten why "I taste" and how it makes him smile, and how it "was hard to find / Oh well, whatever, *Nevermind*."

As for the song's opening guitar riff, it has joined the likes of "Smoke on the Water," "You Really Got Me," and "Dazed and Confused" as one of the most recognizable guitar staples in rock history. "It's totally a dynamic thing," says Kim Thayil, guitar player with Soundgarden and a big admirer of "Teen Spirit." "It's one bass riff, then the guitar changes around that, from heavy to quiet during the guitar solo part. But it was that two-note guitar drone that really stayed with me. I like it when any band does hanging notes like that. Most bands seem to avoid using this technique, perhaps because they don't have the patience to sit there and play one note. Neil Young could, and so he did these one-note solos. But 'Teen Spirit' had everything that song needed dynamically, and it really moved me."

Butch Vig perhaps sums up the song as well as anyone when he says, "I don't know exactly what 'Teen Spirit' means, but you know it means *something*, and it's as intense as hell."

On the back of his tracking sheet for "Smells Like Teen Spirit" Butch Vig attempted to follow Cobain's lyrics. (COURTESY BUTCH VIG)

In Bloom

"In Bloom" had been written a couple of years prior to the *Nevermind* sessions, and a version had been recorded with Chad Channing on drums at Smart Studios. The song is mostly about Kurt's distaste for the macho men of his hometown, Aberdeen. Kurt related the story behind "In Bloom" on *Nevermind: It's an Interview.* "Obviously, I don't like rednecks," he said. "I don't like macho men. You know, I don't like abusive people. I guess that's what that song is about. It's an attack on them."

During the "In Bloom" session, Vig was meticulously attempting to get a good vocal take out of Kurt that he could use as the master, and to that end he ran tape during this entire part of the sessions. "Kurt basically had no patience," Vig recalls. "He wanted to do something in one take and then move on to the next thing. It wasn't really a matter of him not wanting to sing that song anymore, but he would sing so hard, he would frequently blow his voice out after three or four takes."

Kurt's reliable vocal phrasing on the verses from one take to the next allowed Vig to edit together a complete song, overdub, and beef up the chorus. "I just took the best bits from three or four vocal takes and sewed them together." The seamless sonic embroidery worked perfectly.

Cobain's singing became progressively "harder" during recording for "In Bloom." This made it difficult to balance the levels between the song's verses and choruses. "Typically, he would sing sometimes really quietly and then really loud," says Vig. "So I was forced to change the input level as we were recording him on the fly! It's kind of scary because you've got to know the song really well. Then you have to hope he doesn't change the phrasing or do something different."

A problem arose when the band attempted to doubletrack the chorus. The phrasing of Kurt's two tracks was definitely off the mark, as he sang "He's the one / who likes all the pretty songs. . . ." "Kurt was singing for a couple of beats longer on one version versus the other," explains Vig. To remedy the problem, the producer pulled the fader down to cut off the longer take, so the timing of the twin choruses would match.

Cobain's vocals were not the only problem encountered while trying to cut "In Bloom." Grohl was enlisted to sing high harmonies in the chorus. "I was laughing with Dave a lot because the part was just a little out of his range, and his voice kept breaking up," remembers Vig. "He would finish one chorus and light up a cigarette to catch his breath."

Track 17 of "In Bloom" was devoted to recording the guitar part. Kurt used the Mesa Boogie amp for his guitar part on the verses, then he switched to the Fender Bassman on track 18 to achieve a heavier, doubletracked fuzz sound on the chorus. The Mesa had been Kurt's pick, while the Bassman was suggested by Butch. "Kurt was using the Mesa live in concert at the time," Vig remembers. "The Bassman is one of my favorites. To me, the Bassman always defined what grunge was, because it had a really heavy, thick sound with the distortion really saturated at the low end." Recalling Kurt's solo on the track, Vig remarked, "It's pure genius. He just bends the notes so beautifully. 'Solo' is not even the right term—interlude or guitar break is better." The new "In Bloom" was not only more adventurous than the Smart take; it also took on a far-reaching pop melody that would endear it to Nirvana's audience as one of the fans' favorites. Novoselic says that at the time of the Sound City sessions, "In Bloom" was the song the band thought was going to be the first single. "It was such a pop song," he says.

The subsequent popularity of this recording after its release bothered Kurt, as, ironically, a new audience of college jocks and pumped-up "macho men" would sing along at Nirvana's live shows. Kurt's lyric "knows not what it means" had proved unintentionally prophetic.

Come As You Are

"Come As You Are" was another strong yet lyrically confused track. For Nevermind: It's an Interview, Kurt explained: "The lines in the song are really contradictory. You know, one after another. They're just kind of confusing, I guess. It's just about people and what they're expected to act like."

The recording, which starts with Kurt's solo guitar for the first eight seconds, opens with the first verse in a low, moody style, and then the chorus explodes at full volume and locks in the listener. This musical style—dynamic changes between quiet and raucous passages—perfectly complements the conflicting lyrical phrases. It was a style that Nirvana would use on many of their songs.

The enchanting sound made by Cobain's guitar is murky enough to make it seem as if he's playing underwater. Cobain used only a few special effects for his guitar on Nevermind, but "Come As You Are" featured the most obvious one. Vig explains: "He had an Electro-Harmonix Small Clone. That's the watery sound you hear on the guitar in the verse and pre-chorus buildup."

Cobain rarely took an extended guitar solo in the studio, but "Come As You Are" featured one of the longest ones he ever put on record. When the red light went on for Kurt to play his solo, Kurt began the first pass at his part. Although it was good, it just didn't feel right to him. He called up to Butch in the control booth and asked to do it again. The light went on again, and this time he nailed it. "Kurt really did not play a lot of solos," says Vig. "This one is more of a melodic part based on the vocal melody. It's not trying to show off pyrotechnics. It complements the melody of the song."

There were only three vocal takes recorded for "Come As You Are." Take 1 was the best. Then Kurt was asked to doubletrack the vocal part all through the entire song. "It was really close," says the producer. "Usually, when a singer doubletracks his vocals, it's hard to get the phrasing the same. But I put both of them up on the monitors and listened to the two takes, side by side, and it just sounded great."

During the harmony overdub session, Kurt made a small mistake that would remain on tape. After Kurt's guitar solo, one hears Kurt sing "Memori—a" four consecutive times. While tracking the harmony part, Kurt entered early, singing, "And I don't have a gun," underneath the fourth "Memori—a." Butch calls it Kurt's "ghost vocal." "He just came in too early and then he decided to keep it." Like the mistake that was kept in the recording of "Polly," this "error" made for a more distinctive song.

One final touch was tagged onto the song's conclusion in the later mixing stage. Vig decided to sample Kurt's singing of "Memori—a" from a point in the middle of the song. Then he placed it at the end of the song's run-out, twice in the last eight bars. It can be found subtly buried in the mix.

As for the song's lyrics, Cobain seemed to imply that he was no longer going to be judgmental. He sings, "I want you to be / As a friend . . . As an old enemy." The lyrical paradoxes come side by side, suggesting that the singer is resigned to accepting people as they are—whether or not they meet his expectations. Cobain explained to one journalist, "I always knew to question things. All my life, I never believed most things I read in history books and a lot of things I learned in school. But now I've found I don't have the right to make a judgment on someone based on something I've read. I don't have the right to judge anything. That's the lesson I've learned." In many ways, "Come As You Are" represented a newly mature form of songwriting for Cobain, more metaphorical, less direct.

Throughout the *Nevermind* sessions, the atmosphere was fairly relaxed. The band was loose, and tracking went smoothly for the most part. "They were going out all night and partying," says Vig. "I think they had a certain sense of, 'We can do whatever we want!'" On a typical day, Vig would arrive first, at around noon or one o'clock, to set up for the session. The band would arrive, ready to play, at three or four o'clock in the afternoon. Recording sessions typically ran until eleven o'clock or midnight. Once the band had left for the day, Vig remained behind to review the day's progress. He often listened to the multitracks from that day to select the most appropriate passages for use on the finished master. He

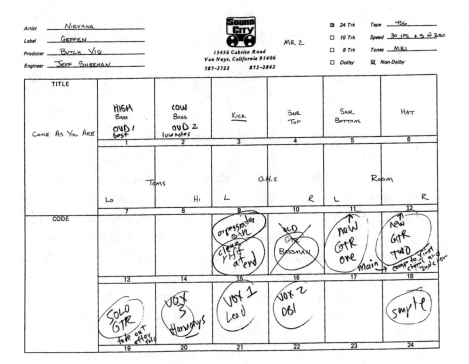

The tracking sheet shows the following handwritten information:

Artist: Nirvana
Label: Geffen
Producer: Butch Vig
Engineer: Jeff Sheehan

Sound City — MR 2
15456 Cabrito Road
Van Nuys, California 91406
787-3722   873-2842

- ☒ 24 Trk — Tape: 456
- ☐ 16 Trk — Speed: 30 IPS + 5 @ 250
- ☐ 8 Trk — Tones: MRI
- ☐ Dolby — ☒ Non-Dolby

TITLE: Come As You Are

HIGH Bass OUD 1 best (1)	LOW Bass OUD 2 low notes (2)	Kick (3)	Snr Top (4)	Snr Bottom (5)	Hat (6)
Lo (7)	Toms Hi (8)	O.H.s L (9)	R (10)	Room L (11)	R (12)

CODE

arpeggiator gtr clean rhythm at end (13)	(14)	OLD gtr BASSMAN (15)	new gtr one Main (16)	new gtr two come to first chorus and 2nd c'rus (17)	(18)
SOLO gtr fade out after solo (19)	VOX 3 Harmonys (20)	VOX 1 Lead (21)	VOX 2 OBI (22)	(23)	smpte (24)

utilized his own expertise as a drummer, listening to Dave and Krist's rhythm parts to make sure they "locked in" with each other.

Vig described his nightly task of selecting from Kurt's alternate vocal takes as a job that posed a unique challenge to him as the producer: "I would go through and pick the best bits from different takes. That's typically how I like to work with a vocalist." However, Kurt would occasionally change lyrics between different vocal takes, which did not make the producer's job any easier. "On some of the songs he did sing some different lines. Sometimes he'd do a take and then come in and listen to it and say, 'I don't like that verse. I'm going to use this one instead,'" admits Vig. When flaws were uncovered, Vig would be set up for the next day's session to punch-in any necessary sonic repairs.

Butch Vig's tracking sheet—essentially a map of the recording—for the song "Come As You Are." (Courtesy Butch Vig)

Breed

"Breed" started out under the title "Immodium," the name the song had been given during the Smart sessions. However, a scratch-out on the tracking sheet indicates the change to its permanent title (naming a song after the trademarked diarrhea medication would have most likely meant a lawsuit). "Breed" is an example of one of Cobain's many compositions where the title of the song is buried deep within the lyrics—in this case not appearing until the song is halfway over. The tune was designed to capture the mood of many a middle-class teen trapped by fear and apathy. To drive home this point, Kurt sings, "I don't care" five consecutive times within a single-note verse. He follows later with repetitious lines of "I don't mind," "Get away," and "I'm afraid." On *Nevermind: It's an Interview*, Kurt described the sentiment of hopelessness conveyed in this song: "I was helpless when I was twelve, when Reagan got elected, and there was nothing I could do about that. But now this generation is growing up, and they're in their mid-twenties; they're not putting up with it." Kurt's sentiments about Reaganism support one rock critic's theory that no landmark album has ever been recorded when the liberal party has been in power in the United States—that it takes a conservative, status-quo government to drive artists to rebel and craft great rock 'n' roll.

Musically, this fast-paced 4/4 rocker begins with a long, low guitar hum. Kurt leads in with a quick six-note guitar solo, which repeats two times before Dave Grohl's drum roll barrage attacks the listener like machine gun bursts from an Uzi. The drum sound, which locks in on Krist's bass line as of the fifth measure, is powerful, crisp, in-your-face punk music. At the end of this monstrous musical buildup, Kurt starts to scream.

"Breed" prominently featured Dave Grohl pounding away on the Terminator snare drum. The Drum Doctor vividly recalls watching Grohl play on this recording: "I remember Dave with his long hair—it just looked like a big pile of hair when he was playing the drums. His head was just moving all the time with the music. And it was just flinging all his dark hair around."

For the "Breed" sessions Vig repeated a technique he had used on the version recorded one year earlier at Smart Studios. As Kurt tears into a set of solo riffs, Butch flies them quickly left to right. Thus the guitar sound soars from the right channel, up to center, and over to the left channel as the riff fades. Quickly, another riff takes flight again, with the same dizzying dynamic motion. The movement of sound between the channels causes the listener to focus more intently on the music. The sonic effect was reminiscent of the jet engine sound employed by producer George Martin at the beginning of the Beatles song "Back in the U.S.S.R."

One of the recording techniques Butch had developed back home at Smart Studios was a drum tunnel. The tunnel was used on all of *Nevermind*'s drum tracks except "Polly" and "Something in the Way." Its punchy sound is crucial to the pulsing bass drum hits Grohl plays on "Breed" and other tracks. Butch revealed the technical secret behind his innovative drum sound: "It's something that I have at Smart that I've used on and off. Basically, you can take a drum shell and extend it as long as you want. We extended Dave Grohl's bass drum out an additional six feet. You can put Velcro straps and some padding around the shell to seal the connection."

The next step was the all-important placement of the drum mikes and the blending of different sounds. Butch explains, "I typically put a Sennheiser 421 or an Electrovoice RE 20 close to the batter bass drum head. Then I put an FET 47 microphone about five feet away." And, just as an artist mixes colors on his palette, Vig blended the sound of the two mikes together on the recording. In this way, he was able to prevent the pick-up of extraneous room sound while getting more low-end (or thump, to use the parlance) from the kick against the bass drum. The live feel of the "Breed" drum sound derives much from the drum tunnel. As you listen to the song, you can almost feel the thump in your chest as if you were listening to the band live in front of a concert stage. Butch typically downplays the significance of his recording technique. "I didn't really think that anything I was doing was that special. Just common sense. It's not like I had some formula or something. It probably just comes from my background of not having much gear. I've never really been that particular, like having to use a specific bass drum mike, because I did so many records in studios where you used whatever you had."

Kurt made four vocal passes on "Breed." As his producer recalls, each succeeding take "kept getting worse because he blew his voice out." Unique to "Breed" was Vig's use of a U89 Neuman microphone for Kurt's vocals. "At the time, I thought of using this one [rather than a U67] because he was singing higher and pushing the limits of his voice up. I just thought we needed more body to it." The U89 is a microphone used for recording higher-frequency sounds. Kurt's first vocal take was selected as the master.

Lithium

The recording session for "Lithium" was one of the most arduous for Butch and the band. The lyrics are filled with images of Kurt's past, appropriate for a song named after a prescription antidepressant. The protagonist struggles with themes of happiness, insecurity, loneliness, religion, and sanity throughout. It was one of the few songs that Cobain would admit he worked hard to complete, approaching it with a greater concern for meaning than other work. "[It's] just a story that I made up," he told Patrick MacDonald in 1991. "It was one of the songs I actually did finish while trying to write it instead of taking pieces of my poetry and other things."

Not only was it a hard song for Kurt to write, it also provided one of the biggest struggles during the recording of *Nevermind*. Despite the stress and adversity involved in completing this song, the session would yield a second song called "Endless, Nameless."

Early on, the producer struggled with instrumental portions of "Lithium." He explains, "First of all, they kept speeding the song up. It was one of the few tracks that we used a click-track to." (A click-track is an automated rhythm sound device used to keep a drummer's timing at a consistent tempo.) Continuing, Vig recalls, "Dave was great. He'd never really worked with one, but he was fine as soon as he did it a couple of times." Butch and the band then suggested some simpler fills and patterns for Dave to play on "Lithium." The experiment worked well, with the band finally laying down the instrumental track.

Cobain's part, however, took quite a bit of time to perfect. "Kurt wanted to be able to play the guitar very . . . *not* methodical—it needed to have this space," says Vig. "It had to be very relaxed." But when the guitar began to speed up, Vig would call for another take. With each successive take, Kurt's fuse grew shorter. Vig also did some guitar overdubbing to achieve the live-sounding dynamic that the band wanted. But the process was painfully slow that day. "We'd get a sound for the verse and then work on the chorus sections," the producer reflects.

They recorded only two vocal takes of the verses to "Lithium." Overall, take 2 was the best performance and was the one that was used. In reviewing both takes side by side, Vig decided to take the second line of the second verse from Kurt's first vocal pass and drop it in to the master vocal take. The vocal chorus was then quickly recorded live and doubletracked.

To achieve the thumping, darker sound on "Lithium," the band employed an Electro-Harmonix Big Muff fuzz box through a Fender Bassman amplifier. "As I recall," says Vig, "we used a U87 microphone on that. We wanted something that was not so bright, a heavier sound." The U87 was a microphone that the producer usually reserved for capturing low-frequency instruments like bass guitar. Two tracks were devoted to Krist's bass part. An additional three tracks recorded Kurt's guitar, all gauged to beef up the sound.

The band's style at the time of *Nevermind* frequently contrasted the dynamics of a low, relaxed groove with a hellacious, loud grunge barrage. It was not easy to combine such different, dynamic sounds. "Getting the verses to sound relaxed and the chorus to sound as intense as possible, and make the transitions feel natural and effortless, was a hard one to do," admits Vig.

Endless, Nameless

Recalling the first difficult day of recording "Lithium," Butch describes how a breakdown caused the birth of "Endless, Nameless." "I remember the first day we were cutting it. Kurt got really pissed off because it was taking too much time." Acknowledging Kurt's lack of patience, Vig wisely kept the tapes rolling as the band launched into a jam they had rehearsed in different forms months before the session. Cobain's moodiness—both in the studio and at live performances—was well documented by associates and the rest of the band, so his "Lithium" frustration wasn't anything new. "Kurt was such a complex personality," Grohl told *Hit Parader* in 1997. "He could be incredibly warm and funny, and the next moment he could just become totally absorbed in thought. I don't think any of us truly understood what was going on inside his head."

On this day, however, Kurt's feelings were obvious to everyone present in the studio. "During 'Endless, Nameless,'" says Butch, "Kurt was *really* pissed off, thrashing and screaming, and he smashed his guitar in the middle of it." The band continued to play through the death of Cobain's guitar (which can be heard around the nineteen-and-one-half-minute mark of the last CD track). Kurt ran back to the microphone to scream some barely audible words. Reflecting back on smashing his guitar, Kurt explained simply, in the home video *Live! Tonight! Sold Out!*, "You get satisfaction, climax." In the aftermath of this apocalyptic recording, the producer calmly recalls telling the band, "Okay, well, I guess we'd better go out and find a left-handed [Mosrite] . . . [laughing] because we can't record any more guitar today." (Others at the session remember the guitar being a Fender.)

Later that evening, Vig went back to Sound City to review the day's tapes. Kurt's shattered guitar was still in a heap as Vig filled out the tracking sheet for "Endless, Nameless." It was the only tracking sheet from the session that wouldn't be covered with marked-out notations, since it was the only one done after a session had ended. The entire recording had been made live with no overdubs. Kurt's "scratch" vocal and guitar were recorded from the center of the room (a "scratch" is a vocal take done to show placement—it is not meant to be used in the finished product). The spontaneity of this track is evidenced by Cobain's use of a Shure 57 microphone, normally set up for talkback to the control room. This microphone was designed for conversation—not music—and was intended to be used only for the musicians to communicate with the control room. Unlike the other microphones used for recording, which were directional and didn't pick up the other noises in the room, this Shure recorded everything else in the room. "We had tremendous bleed from the bass and drums all pouring into Kurt's microphone on that one," recalls Vig.

Never seriously considered as part of the album's original running order, the omission of the song's title from the album sleeve was purposeful. The relatively new technology of the compact disc, with its increased storage capacity, prompted the band to hide this lengthy aural nightmare. The group did not want the album to end with the dreamy, quiet "Something in the Way." They also knew if the last song had several minutes of silence following "Something," that one of two things might happen: listeners would either turn off the CD player manually and never hear the song; or they would let the player continue and get the shock of their lives when "Endless, Nameless" crashed into their living room after ten minutes of silence. "It was kind of a joke for the band to do, as in, 'We're not going to list it in the packaging, or [mention] it exists,'" Geffen's vice president of marketing, Robert Smith, told ICE in 1991. "It's for that person who plays the CD, it ends, they're walking around the house, and ten minutes later . . . kaboom!"

Dave Grohl recounted the band's motives on *Nevermind: It's an Interview*: "I think the original reason for it was because 'Something in the Way' is sort of your slow song. It's the last song on the record and most likely to be listened to by someone who would have a carousel CD player. So, why not screw up their little carousel deal?" Vig was an enthusiastic supporter of the band's hidden-track concept. His own band, Spooner had done the very same thing during the 1980s. "Even going back to Spooner's *Wildest Dreams* album," says Butch, "we had a lot of little ear candy on there. Between songs there were little snippets of things. You can have the regular body of music and there is all this extra time [on CDs]. So you might as well put *something* in there."

Polly

"Polly" was the only recording from the abandoned Smart Studios session that made it onto *Nevermind*, though the album credits fail to mention details of the Madison session. The song was used exactly as originally recorded at Smart, and, according to Vig, it was not rerecorded at Sound City. It is the only track on the album to feature an uncredited Chad Channing, who had left the band one year prior to the release of *Nevermind*. "It's the same song," confirms Novoselic. "Chad never got credit on *Nevermind* for that."

Veteran sound mixer Andy Wallace, who was called in after all the *Nevermind* recordings were finished, had the responsibility of blending the sounds of "Polly" so it would fit in with the other songs on the album. "Polly" also presented some problems for Wallace because it was the only song he worked with that was recorded on sixteen-track equipment—all the Sound City songs were on twenty-four-track. It required that Wallace use a special machine to mix it.

One of the techniques Wallace used on *Nevermind* was to add a "delay line effect," which gave Channing's cymbal crashes on "Polly" their haunting shimmer. Wallace explains: "It's not like an echo because the time span is shorter. It offsets the time [on the cymbal hit] just a slight bit from the original, blends them together, and then changes that offset. So there is a slight pitch wobble going on." Used sparingly, but with a purpose, Wallace was able to add shading and drama to a great recording. In recalling Nirvana's work on "Polly," Wallace says, "That song had a great sound to it."

Territorial Pissings

To state that the lyrics to "Territorial Pissings" combine a number of disjointed themes is to understate the obvious. The title itself—with its suggestion of urination used to mark residency—conveys further evidence of Kurt's disdain for macho poseurs. Like "Polly," "In Bloom," and the earlier song "Mr. Moustache," the song can be seen as an attack on traditional male stereotypes. Still, trying to make anything important out of this experimental lyric may be asking too much, because at different points in the song Kurt muses about feminism, paranoia, and even being an alien from outer space. "At the time I was writing those songs," Kurt said in a 1992 interview, "I really didn't know what I was trying to say. There's no point in my even trying to analyze or explain it." The song kicks off with Krist Novoselic's sarcastic a cappella rendition of the song "Get Together," which had been a hit for the Youngbloods two decades earlier.

Prior to the *Nevermind* sessions, "Territorial Pissings" had been played only once live, and that debut did not feature the Youngbloods intro. When the band began working on the song in the studio, they wanted to place something at the start of the song, before the punk barrage kicked in. Kurt suggested to Vig, "Maybe we should put some kind of vocal thing on there?" Vig turned to Krist and said, "Why don't you go in and sing some song you think is really lame?" Krist enthusiastically replied, "Okay. How about this?" He began singing the lyrics to "Get Together." Vig thought it was perfect. Krist's sarcastic rendering of the Youngblood's lyric ("Everybody get together / Try to love one another right now") is striking as juxtaposed to Kurt's repetitive chorus, which speaks to the loss of ideals ("Gotta find a way / A better way"). It also suggests a sarcastic message from Krist and Kurt to their respective estranged parents, whose generation espoused the ideals of brotherly and sisterly love but whose own marriages more often than not ended up in divorce. "I wanted to put some kind of corny hippie idealism in it," Novoselic told Michael Azerrad. "Maybe it was about lost ideals."

After the band had given the song a couple of run-throughs and it came time to run tape, Vig asked Cobain what the title of this new song might be. Kurt told Butch, "Call it the 'Punk Song.'" So the producer dutifully wrote "Punk Song" on the track sheet and left it there until Cobain later came up with a better title. Cobain wanted to plug his electric guitar directly into the producer's mixing board to get a pure punk sound, but Vig was not entirely convinced that this was such a great idea. In the end, they struck a compromise. Butch relates the story: "Kurt wanted to plug straight into the desk for a trashy punk sound, but I didn't think the guitar had any balls. So we actually split the signal between an amplifier and plugged Kurt's Pro Co Rat distortion pedal directly into the Neve control board and blended both into the final mix." Cobain recorded three takes on guitar. Take 3 was circled as "best" on the producer's track sheet.

Cobain was able to achieve his desired goal, creating an apocalyptic, sheared-edge, distorted guitar sound. The easygoing producer accommodated Kurt because the resulting track coincided with his own philosophy. "I prefer to get the guitars as in-your-face as possible," says Vig. Recording the song in this unorthodox fashion was the ultimate tribute to the lo-fi punk records Kurt and Krist had listened to in their youth.

Once it came time to record the vocals, Kurt sang a scratch vocal to warm up. Then he got on the talkback intercom to Vig in the control room and announced, "Butch, I'm only going to sing one take on this. I'm *not* going to do anymore!" Having heard the scratch vocal, Vig understood that Kurt was planning to expend an entire day's vocal cords belting out the words to "Punk Song." There would be nothing but a broken warble at the end.

After Krist's vocal intro, we hear the brief sound of guitar noodlings, followed quickly by an ear-splitting speed-metal riff that makes the listener think their speakers are about to blow out. As the guitar churns its speed-of-light riffs, accompanied by accelerated drum rolls, Kurt prepares for his vocal entrance with a snarling guttural growl reminiscent of the late Doors singer, Jim Morrison. A break in the middle of the song gives the listener (and Kurt) a breather as Grohl pounds out the measures with a simple yet powerful solo. After the solo, Kurt crashes back into the song, repeating the chorus in alternating lyrical screams.

As assistant engineer Doug Olson had remarked after the Smart sessions, "Kurt could definitely scream on key." "Territorial Pissings" ends with Cobain shredding his vocal cords in dramatic fashion. "One reason Kurt would blow his voice out," remembers Vig, "was [because] he was singing hard. He would sing the verse a certain way and usually come to the chorus, and if he was singing really hard, he would totally blow his voice out every time."

"Territorial Pissings" later served as a popular closer for Nirvana's live shows—and just like the studio recording, live performance frequently meant the end of Kurt's vocal abilities for the night.

Drain You

Four power chords provide the musical framework for "Drain You." The track is a pure and simple punk rock love song. Unlike the other songs found on *Nevermind*, "Drain You" does not contain lyrical ambiguity or contradictory images—its themes of love and dependence are quite straightforward. Cobain graphically describes the depth of his affections for his romantic partner. In the lyrics, he offers to "Chew your meat for you / Pass it back and forth / In a passionate kiss / From my mouth to yours / 'Cause I like you."

"Drain You" was one of the few songs done at Sound City that had not been rehearsed previously in Tacoma. "That song we put together when we were rehearsing in Los Angeles with Butch," Novoselic recalls.

Cobain tried several experiments with different guitars and amps before arriving at the right sound combination for this song. At first, he recorded two takes of the song using his Mesa Boogie amp and different guitars. "The early passes sounded scratchy and grating," reflects Vig. "And the way he was playing didn't sound very good." Next, Kurt tried the Bassman amp and ran his Rat pedal effect into it for yet another recording experiment. Again, the first take was rejected, but the next two takes were keepers. The producer used both in the final mix.

Vig coaxed Cobain into singing three vocal takes for "Drain You." Take 2 was chosen as the lead vocal on the verses, while take 1 was used as the master on the chorus. Take 3 did not go to waste, however, as Vig used Kurt's singing of the lyrics "poison apple" for the harmonies.

While recording his vocals during the instrumental solo section of the song, Kurt started making weird noises into the microphone. He had not told his producer in advance what he was going to do. "I just let the song roll," says Vig. "He was doing some of these things with his mouth and some with his hands right up close to the microphone." After completing his third take, Kurt told Butch, "Hey, don't erase those things, because I want to use them in the middle." The mix ultimately used all three takes of weird squeaky noises during Dave's solo passage, a technique that years earlier marked Patti Smith's "Birdland."

Grohl's drumming plays a key role in the middle of this song. As Kurt repeats the word "you" five times in a dreamy sequence, the band slips into an extended instrumental passage which features a Grohl drum solo. Dave's hypnotic groove seems to borrow its sound from a traditional Native American rain dance. It builds slowly, gaining momentum with Kurt's guitar antiflourishes, until the crescendo crashes headlong back into a repetitive four-chord structure and Kurt's bloodcurdling scream. While downplaying his own work as a guitarist, Kurt, in a 1992 interview, explained the important role Dave and Krist played in developing the song's feel: "While I can do a lot by switching channels on my amp, it's Dave who really brings the physicality to the dynamics," Cobain told journalist Chuck Crisafulli. "Krist is great at keeping everything going along at some kind of even keel. I'm just the folk singer in the middle."

Despite the success "Teen Spirit" would ultimately enjoy, Cobain cited "Drain You" as one song that he preferred as a songwriter, telling *Rolling Stone*, "I think there are so many other songs that I've written that are as good, if not better, than that song ['Teen Spirit'], like 'Drain You.'" The overplay received by "Teen Spirit" on radio and MTV undoubtedly influenced Kurt's opinion to some degree, though he was passionate in touting "Drain You." "I love the lyrics," he told *Rolling Stone*. "And I never get tired of playing it." Though Cobain never definitively explained who or what the song was about, it's worth noting that he wrote "Drain You" three months after meeting Courtney Love. The band debuted the song live at the first full concert they did after finishing the album, in San Francisco on June 13, 1991. From that point on, Nirvana included the song in every full concert but one (San Francisco on April 9, 1993), and, along with "School," it became the most played Nirvana song, frequently leading off their concerts.

Lounge Act

"Lounge Act" is a showcase for Krist Novoselic's inventive, melodic bass lines, and his solo bass riff starts out the song. Kurt told Nirvana biographer Michael Azerrad, "That song is mostly about . . . having a certain vision and being smothered by a relationship and not being able to finish what you wanted to do artistically because the other person gets in your way." The concept for the title came from Kurt and Krist's thinking that the music sounded typical of a lounge bar band.

Cobain laid down two guitar tracks using the Bassman amp, one clean and one highly distorted. He then sang a scratch vocal, followed by three formal vocal passes. He decided to add some drama and urgency to his vocal performance, and in the first two verses of the song he half sings, half speaks the lyrics. However, in the third verse Kurt sings and screams at an octave above his normal range. The result is another angst-ridden performance with Kurt straining his vocal cords yet again. The song ends with the sound of a long, straight guitar tone. A proper ending would not be completed until the final mixing session. Though this song wasn't played live until August 20, 1991, in Cork, Ireland, Chad Channing says he remembers this tune being rehearsed years earlier, used by the band as a goof-around during practices.

Stay Away

"Stay Away" was another song that Kurt had been holding on to for more than a year. In its earlier incarnation, the band had recorded a version at Smart Studios under the title "Pay to Play." The Sound City track sheets show that the name "Stay Away" did not surface until recording was already under way. In the year since the band had recorded the song at Smart, Cobain was able to revise and refocus the lyrics, giving them new meaning.

The song's genesis may well have come from the rough treatment Kurt received in his hometown. Kurt explained in a 1992 interview: "I got beat up a lot, of course, because of my association with them [gays]. People just thought I was weird at first, just some fucked-up kid. But once I got the gay tag, it gave me the freedom to be able to be a freak and let people know that they should just stay away from me. Instead of having to explain to someone that they should just stay the fuck away from me— I'm [thought to be] gay, so I can't even be touched." His angry repetition of the words "Stay Away" throughout the song reinforces a feeling of alienation and distance between the author and his targeted audience.

Production notes for this song indicate that the band used the same technical setup that they used for "Breed." The band recorded the instrumental backing live, while Kurt sang lead. Then Kurt played a second guitar lead with his Mesa amp, which Vig sparingly overdubbed onto the master guitar part. "It was meant to sound like one guitar versus an overdub with two split guitars," the producer says. Vig was able to blend Kurt's voice and guitar (sounding like an engine whine) for the passage "I don't know why." The effect created the illusion, with its tortured string bends, that Kurt's guitar had been surgically implanted into his vocal cords.

Getting the vocals to match up with the guitar part posed a unique challenge. Kurt had recorded two passes at "Pay to Play" that were left abandoned on tracks 19 and 20. He then reworked the lyrics significantly and asked Butch to scratch out the old title and write in "Stay Away." Two more vocal takes of "Stay Away" were cut, and Kurt thought he was finished. "He was doing it live, singing and playing the chords," Vig remembers. "He'd do the little [string] bends but always have a tough time singing 'I don't know why' and then [getting] back to the chords and verse." So Vig suggested to Kurt that he overdub just that one line. The overdub was placed alone on track 15. Once Kurt had recorded the key line, he told Butch, "Let's make this razor sharp. Just in your face and then gone!" Vig took the overdub vocal part and put it into a sampler. "I went in and shifted it around and got the vocal so it matched the guitar part perfectly. It's like someone goes in and pushes a button [singing], 'I don't know why,' and cuts out, super tight and pinpointed so it hits you in the face."

On a Plain

One of the last songs Kurt Cobain wrote before going in to record *Nevermind* was "On a Plain." The song is pure pop, with great hooks placed throughout. Again, the lyrics are open to different interpretations. The obvious reference to be drawn from the title could be to Nirvana's recently elevated lifestyle. At the time of the *Nevermind* sessions, however, the band was still living in poverty, even if that poverty was broken up by cross-country trips to be wined and dined by record labels. "On a Plain" could also simply be a metaphor for being high, and indeed the second line of the song is, "I got so high that I scratched 'til I bled." Later in the song Kurt consciously decides to cover up the more personal references, and he sings "It is now time / To make it unclear."

When in 1993 Jon Savage asked Cobain what the track was about, the singer replied, "Classic alienation, I guess." But for this song, like others he was asked about over the years, his own personal explanation could be called into question, as he himself noted. "Every time I go through songs I have to change my story, because I'm as lost as anyone else," he told Savage. "For the most part, I write songs from pieces of poetry thrown together. When I write poetry, it's not usually thematic at all. I have plenty of notebooks, and when it comes time to write lyrics, I just steal from my poems."

Setting the input levels for Kurt's all-out electric guitar sound on "On a Plain" was a challenge for Vig, one that he says required techniques he'd experimented with for bands like Killdozer. "I put three mikes on [Kurt's guitar], a 57, a U87, and a 414. Or sometimes a 421. And then I would pick just one of those mikes." These were all mikes that the producer had used in the past, and come to prefer, for recording electric guitar. Moving mikes around and checking sound levels while Kurt was waiting to play was not an easy chore. "He was very impatient," says Vig. So the producer developed a technique to bypass the impatient Cobain before he arrived for the session. "A way I liked to check the mikes was to turn the amp on full blast, but with no guitar plugged in. So you get the hiss coming out of the speaker, which, in essence, is a white-noise signal that you can use to fine tune microphone placement by listening to the phasing. I don't like a lot of room ambience. I prefer the guitars to be really in your face."

Cobain recorded a live guitar part for the song using the "grungy" Bassman amp. Then he added a little bit more guitar on the chorus. Novoselic recorded an ambient-sounding bass part that complements the song's mood.

Vocally, "On a Plain" was one of the easier songs for Kurt to sing on *Nevermind*. He nailed the lead vocal in one take. Unique to the song were Dave's high harmonies at the end of the song. Vig thought Dave's double-tracked harmonies blended so well with Kurt's that he suggested an a cappella coda to round out the song. In the end, the idea would be discarded.

"They did those harmonies another eight times," Vig says. "I wanted to bring the music all the way down and leave those vocals in a cappella for four times, just by themselves. We actually mixed it that way, but when Kurt heard it, he decided he just wanted to hear one pass without music and cut out."

"Something in the Way" occupies the last official track on the album, excluding the hidden song "Endless, Nameless." Written just before the *Nevermind* sessions got under way, it was most likely the last song composed for the album. It was based on the few occasions in late 1985 when young Kurt tried to escape family problems by running away from home and sleeping under the North Aberdeen Bridge. The bridge was a plain structure constructed of wood and concrete that crossed over the Wishkah River. This period of Kurt's life has been mythologized by the media as his "homeless period."

In the song, Kurt fantasized he was a sick, AIDS-infected, homeless street person. He sang, "Underneath the bridge / The tarp has sprung a leak / And the animals I've trapped / Have all become my pets . . ." It was a hard song to write—and it's a hard song to listen to—but Cobain downplayed it when talking about the song with Michael Azerrad, suggesting the song was more a "fantasy" of what it would be like if he were homeless: "That was like if I was living under the bridge and I was dying of AIDS, if I was sick and I couldn't move and I was a total street person. That was kind of the fantasy of it." Cobain did live under the bridge, however briefly, and one is left to wonder how much of the despair in the song was fantasy and how much was real for him.

Vig's job of capturing the purity, loneliness, and emotion of "Something in the Way" would be a challenge. Kurt decided to record the song using his cheap, plunky, old five-string acoustic guitar, the same one heard on "Polly." Novoselic remembers the instrument well. "We bought it for twenty dollars in Denver, Colorado," he says. "Kurt took the twelve strings off and put six strings on it. But it wouldn't stay in tune, so he took the head stock and tightened it as much as he could. He had this pair of pliers and when it would go out of tune he'd put the pliers to the tuning pick. It was a total fucking joke, but it worked for him."

Keeping the guitar reasonably in tune was one problem, but so was recording it. Butch wired Kurt's guitar with an AKG 414 microphone. The acoustic and vocal tracks were first cut live in studio A. The band tried to track the song live, but it wasn't working. The track sheet for "Something" indicates a number of tracks crossed out from the initial recording attempts. In the early takes the requisite emotive sensibility was missing.

After several tries, Butch recalls that Kurt finally walked into the control room in studio A, guitar in hand, and slumped on the couch. "I remember asking Kurt to write the lyrics on the back of the track sheet for me," says Vig. After he had finished writing, Cobain started strumming the riffs of "Something in the Way" and singing the lyrics. "He played his old five-string acoustic, and he *never* tuned, but it had a very unique sound, almost like a ukulele, and it gave the song a lot of character." The mood and feel of Kurt's control-room performance were perfect. "He sang so quietly, almost in a whisper, that you could hear a pin drop. So I unplugged the telephone, turned off the air-conditioning, set up mikes and we recorded the vocal and acoustic right there, three takes on the couch." You can actually hear each breath emitted by Kurt as he sings the song in the control room. Vocal take 1 was deemed the keeper for the verses. Kurt then overdubbed the chorus, doubletracked it and added his own harmonies.

Recording the vocals and guitar ahead of the bass and drums posed a final technical challenge to Vig. Krist's bass, Dave's drums, and the harmonies were overdubbed in studio B, one of the few times the band used the smaller studio down the hall from Sound City's big room. It took quite a bit of time to get the drums right on "Something." Vig continually pleaded with the powerful Grohl to "play wimpy" in order to match the mood of the song. "Kurt and I wanted the drums to be *very* understated," says Butch. "Dave was used to playing much louder; plus, it can be very difficult to go back and lay drums over an acoustic guitar track, as the meter may vary a bit. In the end, Dave came up with a great performance."

Grohl would eventually have his way once Nirvana went on tour in support of *Nevermind*. When the band played "Something in the Way" in concert, he would hit the skins and crash the cymbals hard during the chorus, causing his entire drum kit to rock from the force. "The real core of any tenderness or rage is tapped the very second that a song is written," Cobain told Chuck Crisafulli. "It's . . . sort of [a] dishonesty that you can never recapture the emotion of a song completely performing in sports arenas." This thinking may explain why "Something in the Way" became an entirely different song when played live by the band ("We had this big arrangement we threw into it," Novoselic says), and though it was emotional, it never recaptured the power of the track on *Nevermind*.

Krist recorded two takes of the bass line. "Even that was difficult to sync up with Kurt's part," says Vig. "We had to punch in spots, just so Krist would get the languid feel on the bass to lock up with the acoustics."

The cello was one of the last touches added to "Something in the Way." Kurt explained the idea for his musical arrangement on *Nevermind: It's an Interview:* "I knew I wanted cello on it. After all the music was recorded for it, we'd forgotten about putting a cello on it. We had one more day in the studio and we decided, 'Oh geez, we should try to hire a cellist.' We were at a party, and we were asking some of our friends if they had any friends who play cello, and it just so happened that one of our best friends in L.A. plays cello, so, we took him into the studio on the last day and said, 'Here, play something.' He came up with something right away. It just fell like dominoes—it was really easy."

The friends that Cobain asked were the band L7, and their associate, Kirk Canning, was hired as the cellist. The song was arranged by Vig and Cobain together. The overdub session was tracked in studio B at Sound City, and Canning's cello part was recorded in just two takes. Vig would use the best parts of both takes to create a composite of the beautiful string arrangement.

STAY AWAY

The sessions at Sound City continued, and the band members found themselves hard at work on Memorial Day weekend. They had booked studio A for only sixteen days, and when time ran out they moved over to the smaller studio B to finish up "Something in the Way" and a few other things. At the same time, Ozzy Osbourne, the heavy-metal singer formerly with Black Sabbath and best known for the urban legend that he bit the heads off of live animals onstage (he claimed he hadn't), had moved into Sound City's main room. Osbourne was recording an MTV appearance, pretending to play live in the studio.

Nirvana and their producer decided to celebrate Memorial Day in style by holding an old-fashioned barbecue in the Sound City parking lot in front of studio A. Novoselic took charge and began preparing chicken on the grill. While Butch, Kurt, Dave, and Krist drank beer in the parking lot, Ozzy stepped outside to observe the festivities. "He came out," recalls Butch, "and he just stared at the chicken for about five minutes without saying a word. Nirvana were crowding around him, smiling and giggling. They had all written 'Ozzy' on their knuckles after they first saw him." Finally, a smiling Krist spoke directly to Osbourne, breaking his spaced-out staring spell. "Ozzy, help yourself, man. Dig in if you want some barbecued chicken." Osbourne looked up and stared blankly without responding to Krist or the others (who could hardly contain their laughter) and wandered away. Yet another day at Sound City Studios.

Just as in the movie industry, the process of making a record usually leaves some material on the cutting-room floor. Nirvana, in general, had far fewer outtakes than most bands because when they went into the

Dave Grohl.
(Photograph by Mark Zappasodi)

studio they were well rehearsed and had a clear idea of what they wanted to record. Still, some additional material was recorded at Sound City but discarded by the band during the *Nevermind* sessions. Besides the thirteen titles that made it onto the album, the group recorded three more songs and left a fourth started but never finished.

Sappy

"Sappy" had been recorded by the group at Smart Studios in April 1990. The song was resurrected again at Sound City in late May 1991. "The arrangement we did at Sound City is very close to the Smart version," says Butch. Kurt played the lead guitar part while attempting to sing one live scratch and one formal vocal pass. After overdubbing the lead fuzz guitar with his Rat pedal, Kurt laid down his guitar and walked straight into the control room. "Butch," he said. "I don't want to do this. I'm not into this song right now. So let's just leave it." Vig was disappointed because he had always liked the song's unique melodic structure. "It's kind of a minor [key] thing." He believes the unfinished *Nevermind* version of "Sappy" was the take used to provide the hidden song (track 19) found at the end of the various-artists compilation entitled *No Alternative* (the song is not listed on the packaging and, like "Endless, Nameless," is hidden).

Verse, Chorus, Verse

This is probably the most mysterious unreleased song from the session, surrounded by confusion, at least on the part of Nirvana collectors. Prior to the sessions for *Nevermind*, the band used the names "Sappy" and "Verse, Chorus, Verse" interchangeably for one song, ostensibly the version of "Sappy" recorded at Smart Studios (some Nirvana fans also have identified the song as "Everything and Nothing," adding even more to the confusion). The chorus to this song is, "You're in a laundry room." Starting during the late-1989 Europe tour, the band frequently played this song in concert.

However, Cobain liked the title "Verse, Chorus, Verse" enough, according to Vig, that he also used it on *another* song recorded during the *Nevermind* sessions. The band recorded this new track live. Kurt provided the one and only scratch vocal, which Vig says differed from the lyrics used for "Sappy." Then Kurt overdubbed three guitars to complement the bass and drum parts. Although the song was finished instrumentally, Cobain never recorded a formal lead vocal part, just the rough scratch vocals. The song was then abandoned.

Vig contends that the music and melody were considerably different from those in "Sappy." The fact that the Sound City track sheets show two separate songs on separate days—"Verse, Chorus, Verse" and "Sappy"—confirms this. Also, copyright records show that Cobain (or his agents) registered "Sappy" and "Verse, Chorus, Verse" as different songs. This contradicts the previously held belief among Nirvana fans that there was only one song with two different names. A tape of this song has not been traded among Nirvana collectors, and it remains unreleased (and unfinished).

Old Age

This is another Kurt Cobain composition that was only partially produced during *Nevermind*. The band recorded "Old Age" live, with Kurt again providing a scratch vocal. It was quickly dropped after a guitar overdub was completed. "That one ended up on the first record by Hole," says Butch, referring to the composition (rather than the recording). "I never mixed that one or 'Verse, Chorus, Verse.'"

Song in D

There are no track sheets to reflect that "Song in D" was ever formally recorded. However, it was rehearsed at Sound City. "Kurt was a little leery about this one because it was really jangly," remembers Vig. "I had hoped he would finish the lyrics, because it was an amazing song. It was somewhat like an R.E.M. song." But Kurt told the producer, "I don't want to do this one. It's too poppy." Vig answered, "I don't know, it sounds like a great song. I think you should try and finish it."

Krist Novoselic.
(Photograph by Mark Zappasodi)

Aside from the handful of outtakes that failed to make the final cut, there are an abundance of alternate takes from *Nevermind* that were left in the can. With any album recorded in multitrack, numerous alternate takes usually exist, though the variations of most of the *Nevermind* outtakes are, according to Vig, minor. Vig handed over all alternates and outtakes to Geffen at the conclusion of the session. Perhaps someday, an album's worth of these leftovers will be used for another posthumous Nirvana project.

After the band's several grueling weeks in the studio, *Nevermind* was completely recorded. The budget to produce the album had originally been set for $65,000, but by the time the project was done it cost $120,000—still economical by major-label standards. The budget was a credit to the band's punk ethic of recording quickly and to Butch Vig's background in recording punk records on vastly smaller budgets. When asked about the total expenses for *Nevermind*, Kurt later joked to *Guitar World*'s Jeff Gilbert, "I don't remember, I've got Alzheimer's."

LITHIUM

Once Vig and the band had completed the recordings, it was time for the postproduction phase known as mixing. The job of mixing multitrack tapes involves selecting all the right signals from different instrumental and vocal tracks and coming up with a finished stereo mix. Changing tone, volume, and equalization (EQ) and adding echo, reverb, or doubling instruments and vocals are some of the many options available to a sound mixer.

Vig and Nirvana began mixing *Nevermind* during their time in Sound City's "meat and potatoes" (as Vig described it) studio A. "The Neves are really great consoles and the room is big and live," remarked the producer. At the time, Sound City did not have a digital audiotape (DAT) recorder, so Vig saved his copies of the mixes onto cassette tapes. The original plan had called for the album to be mixed at Devonshire Studios in Burbank, and the crew did temporarily move there, but Vig says, "We only did a few backing vocal tracks and rough mixes of all the songs. I did mix a couple of the songs there with the band, but we weren't happy with them."

It was now early June 1991, and Vig and Nirvana had intended to mix the album without even taking a week off to give the songs—and their ears—a rest, a practice that is customary in the recording industry. Ultimately, the trio and their producer completed a mix of roughly half the songs. Several different mixes were attempted on "Teen Spirit," "Lithium," "Come As You Are," "Something in the Way," and "Endless, Nameless." However, most of these early mixes were not the ones used on the finished *Nevermind*. Butch explains, "The first mixes that we did, before Andy Wallace came in, were really raw, which is how the band wanted them. But to me, I think they sounded too rough."

Cobain and Vig were typically standing side by side in the control room during the early mixing of the album's songs. At one point Vig remembers Cobain telling him, "Take all the high-end off the guitars." Vig argued back, "That would make the guitars sound too muddy." As for the rough vocal mixes, Butch noticed, "There was also a tendency by Kurt to bury the vocals more. [He thought] they sounded cool and were more punk rock that way. I would argue with Kurt: 'Your voice is the most intense thing about the songs, and it deserves to be right up there in your face with the music!'" The mixes at this point didn't sound as focused to Vig as he thought they should.

Comparing those early mixes to the finished *Nevermind* album provides some interesting distinctions between Vig's style and Wallace's subsequent sonic treatment, particularly on "Smells Like Teen Spirit." Vig's guitar tones are, as he describes them, "darker, and not as razor-blade sharp as Wallace's." Novoselic remembers the early "Smells Like Teen Spirit" mix as "amazing." On one early mix of the song, Vig left the ringing, distorted guitar tones that linger after Kurt's solo. As Kurt begins to sing again, the ringing tones remain up in the mix, giving the song a more deranged sensibility, while Kurt's voice is kept a bit below the surface. Wallace's later mix emphasized more balance, bringing out the guitars as well as Kurt's powerful vocal performance.

"When we recorded 'Lithium,' the guitars were dark, very thick in the mid-range, and the snare was much drier-sounding," says Vig. "I left them pretty flat when we EQ'd them in the mix." Wallace's treatment on a few of the songs would prove radically different from Vig's, though on "Something in the Way," and several others, Andy followed Butch's lead. "He stayed faithful to the arrangements and the idea of how the songs were supposed to sound," remarks Vig.

Butch Vig's tape box for his early mixes of *Nevermind*.

Mixing for "Endless, Nameless" went very quickly as Vig turned over the control knobs to the band members themselves and let them have a go at it. "Krist, Dave, and Kurt mixed that song," Vig recalls. "They got behind the board and ran the faders up and down." As the group experimented with the song, Vig told them to do whatever they wanted. "I'm not sure if we mixed it per se," Novoselic says. "It swirls around your head." At the time, Vig had no idea Nirvana was seriously considering including "Endless, Nameless" on the album. "It wasn't until a week or two later, when they went to do the mastering, that Kurt decided he wanted it on," Vig says.

Four or five days into mixing, Gary Gersh and band manager John Silva came over to listen to the songs. The result: a list of mix engineers was sent over for Butch and Nirvana to consider. Though Vig had originally been hired to both produce and mix the record, the sessions had gone on longer than planned. "It wasn't any big deal," says Vig. "We all agreed to get another mix guy in with fresh ears." Butch recalls the meeting with Nirvana over the choices. "I was really excited about the possibility of getting to work with a great engineer, but Kurt looked at the list and, one by one, dismissed them all, saying, 'Scott Litt: don't wanna sound like R.E.M.; Ed Stasium: don't wanna sound like the Smithereens . . .' Until he got to the bottom of the list and saw Andy Wallace's name next to Slayer. Kurt smiled and said, 'Get that guy,' and that's how we hooked up with Andy." Wallace had recently coproduced and mixed Slayer's *Reign in Blood* album, which had a rough and raucous sound to it. Wallace's other credits at the time were probably not ones that Nirvana would have studied, because they included such diverse records as the Doors' *American Prayer*, Run-D.M.C.'s *Raising Hell*, and Madonna's "Into the Groove" remixed single.

Contrary to subsequent media reports, which portrayed Wallace as the mixer chosen by the label and forced on Nirvana, Novoselic reports that the band had no reservations about working with Wallace. "We said, 'Right on,' because those Slayer records were so heavy," Novoselic says. For his part, Wallace did his best to allay any concerns: "By the time we got started, they knew I was not going to bathe them in reverb and polish everything," Wallace says. "They were mainly concerned with making sure there was plenty of bass. I was told to make the sound more thick and beefy, yet discernible."

Andy Wallace mixed
Nevermind.
(COURTESY ANDY
WALLACE)

That he did. The band, Vig, and Wallace moved over to Scream Studios in nearby Studio City to begin the final mix of *Nevermind*. Wallace was faced with treading a fine line between the band's desire for a raw alternative sound and the record company's interest in putting out a product with broad commercial appeal. "Uniformly," Wallace recalls, "we all wanted the recording to sound as big and powerful as possible."

Wallace spent hours listening to instrumental and vocal tracks in various combinations. Vig used his tracking sheet notes to show Wallace which tracks had been selected as best for each song. Because much of the power and excitement of the album came from the drums, Wallace turned down the guitar tracks to isolate the drums and bass, looking for particularly interesting parts to highlight. "I tried to isolate moments that featured things worth featuring, like a certain powerful guitar or drum entrance or a vocal passage," says Wallace. Wallace drew upon his vast experiences, which included mixing hard-rock records in Los Angeles during the '70s and hard-hitting club mixes in New York in the '80s.

One of the effects Wallace used sparingly on *Nevermind* was the subsonic boost, a technique that was popular in dance clubs at the time.

The subsonic effect generated certain low frequencies, adding a more full low-end to the music. Wallace remembers, "I know the guys were real concerned that there be plenty of low-end. Instead of running the whole mix through it, I would have just had it on the side and sent just the low-end material to it, adding that to the mix. However, the degree to which this enhancement was added, if at all, was quite minimal, and it varied from mix to mix."

In searching for the "big, heavy sound," Wallace was working from the mostly live guitars Vig had recorded "au naturel." This presented a bit of a challenge. "Much to Butch and the band's credit," says Wallace, "the album was not *overproduced*. While that was very wise, I think from a structural point of view it made it a little tricky to get it to sound *huge*." For the mixer, the spare production presented problems because, he explains, "I did not have gangs of guitars left and right to work with. Certainly, there were some guitar overdubs. I'm not saying it was just the trio. But there were a few times when I doubled some guitar, but hopefully without violating the type of sound the band did live in concert."

One of the more interesting postproduction flourishes of the sonic paintbrush applied by Andy came at the end of "Lounge Act," the ninth song on *Nevermind*. The song, as recorded, ends on a long, straight guitar tone. Searching for a unique ending without using the standard industry fade-out, Wallace reveals, "We just made the recorder slow down." This effect caused the guitar tone to sound like an engine running out of gas as it slowly comes to a halt.

Recalling the solo passage on "Drain You," which featured Dave's drumming and Kurt's weird noises, Wallace provided some ear candy for those fans who love to listen with headphones. He ran a couple of stereo surround effects with Kurt's noises, so that they travel between the two stereo channels.

Another challenge facing Wallace was the change in dynamics when the guitar, cut live on songs like "Lithium," went from a straight, clean sound to a distorted one as Kurt kicked on a distortion pedal. The effects pedals were kicked live and captured on tape, rather than by the accepted approach of being recorded on a separate track at a different time and edited together. "Sometimes, as you expect with a band playing that thrashing punk style live," Wallace says, "the pedal wouldn't necessarily get hit at exactly the right moment. So I had to do a little finagling there in order to get the hits to come on all at the same time, so the changed sound of the guitar would happen right on the beat of where the drums were."

Andy Wallace provided the sonic shine that would help get *Nevermind* on the radio. He employed techniques that brightened the sounds and brought Kurt's unique vocal style up front where it belonged. "Andy EQ'd things a little bit more," reflects Vig. "The separation is there—things pop out more—and it's a little brighter, and he has a few more effects going on." Wallace's heavy-on-the-low-end mixes pleased the band yet kept the music discernible to listeners. And equally important, Wallace's mixes worked with the production techniques that Vig used, making them an effective combination on this project.

Subsequent to the album's release, however, and after the record became a hit, Cobain began to criticize the mixing. He told Michael Azerrad, "It's such a perfect mixture of cleanliness and nice, candy-ass production. . . . It may be extreme to some people who aren't used to it, but I think it's kind of lame myself." Wallace and Vig are quick to note that at the time, in 1991, the band members loved the mixes, and the group signed off on the finished product. Wallace does not believe the band approved the mixes at the time simply because of pressure from the label. "I don't think that they were being hypnotized by the powers that be at all at the time," he says. "They were not *talked* into liking the mixes." If anything, the success of the album and subsequent attention may have helped "talk" Cobain into *not* liking the mixes.

After *Nevermind*'s release, Wallace's next contact with the band was just after the album had achieved gold record status in late November 1991. He received a telephone call from Cobain, asking him to record, produce, and mix some live Nirvana performances. At the time, Kurt expressed the band's appreciation for *Nevermind*'s production and mix. Wallace believes, however, that *Nevermind*'s overwhelming success may have caused the band to move in a different creative direction. "Kurt certainly got put into a different place because of the huge success of that album," Wallace says. "I think his comments concerning *Nevermind* were not so much to specifically express rejection or dissatisfaction with *Nevermind*, as much as wanting to do something new. I think the guys felt, from their own perspective, that they wanted to get back a little closer to the rootsier *Bleach* idea."

Wallace's explanation foreshadowed the band's subsequent decision to hire producer Steve Albini to record *In Utero*. Albini was well known for his sparse, garage-band style of recording. Ironically, it was Cobain who again sought Wallace's mixing acumen to polish *In Utero* after it was recorded. However, Wallace would not be permitted to take the job, due to contractual provisions granting Albini authority over the *In Utero* mixes.

At the rate of one song per day, *Nevermind's* final mix was completed in a two-week period. All parties involved were physically and emotionally drained. By June's end—just under two months after they began—the album was completely recorded and mixed. The next stage was the mastering of the tapes down from twenty-four tracks to two, for reproduction onto compact discs, vinyl albums, and cassettes.

SAPPY

The mastering process is the last creative step in making a sound recording. It is the final opportunity to "fix" the sounds on an album through studio wizardry. All sorts of tweaks, fades, and even edits can be made during the mastering stage through the use of compression, effects, and
equalization. The mastering engineer takes the multitrack tapes and
processes them down to two stereo tracks. In the process, the mastering
engineer can add a great number of effects and change the sound of an
album dramatically, but the overall goal is to create a record that sounds
as good on home stereos and car speakers as it does in the recording studio. The final result of mastering is usually a digital master tape that is
then sent to the CD pressing plants for reproduction. Vinyl masters are
often cut on the premises for use at record pressing plants. Mastering can
also be a point where artists, technical personnel, and record-label executives take the opportunity to celebrate the end of their labors.

Once Andy Wallace had finished his mix of *Nevermind*, the master
tapes were forwarded to Howie Weinberg at Masterdisk Studios in New
York City. "I'm sort of the goal tender in the creative process," says
Weinberg. "I'm the last stop to make it better before pressing." While
many of the principals who worked on *Nevermind* were novices when it
came to making major-label albums—the band in particular—Weinberg
was a well-known veteran who had mastered many of the greatest albums
of the modern rock era. Some of the many artists for whom he had mastered albums included the Clash, Prince, Slayer, Sonic Youth, and
Aerosmith, to name but a few. Weinberg was selected by DGC, a label
he'd done lots of work for before. He'd also previously worked with Vig,

but never with Nirvana, and the group had little understanding of what the mastering process meant. It was Weinberg's work on the album that created an artistic controversy with the band and turned the first pressing into an instant collector's item.

The session was booked to begin at 1:00 P.M. on the afternoon of August 2, 1991, a hot and humid day in New York. Ready to go at the appointed hour, Weinberg found himself all alone in the studio. There was no sign of the band or record-label representatives. Because the *Nevermind* master tapes were already there, he began work on them by himself. Weinberg recalls how the session proceeded: "I start working whether the clients are there or not. *Nevermind* sounded like a pretty cool alternative record to me. When I put it on, I got all charged up. I began listening to it and working on it. Two o'clock rolled around, no one showed up, then three o'clock, four o'clock. No one there, just me working all alone. So I got the sounds just right. Then, five o'clock, everybody shows up. Andy Wallace, Gary Gersh, and Nirvana. So I said, 'Guess what? I've got most of it done.'"

The assembled party settled in to listen. Weinberg pushed "play" and the tape began to resonate with Kurt's crisp, lurching guitar riffs on

NEVERMIND/NIRVANA

"Teen Spirit." When the album had played through, Weinberg sat back in his studio chair to await the response. He recalls, "Their reaction was, 'Wow, it sounds great.' Everybody loved it. We did a few more things, and it was basically done."

During the session, Weinberg had mastered the song "Endless, Nameless," but may not have realized it was meant for the album, especially since it lacked the tighter focus of the other tracks. When asked whether the band had communicated their desire to create a hidden track with "Endless, Nameless," Weinberg explains, "In the beginning, it was kind of a verbal thing to put that track at the end. Maybe I misconstrued their instructions, so you can call it my mistake if you want. Maybe I didn't write it down when Nirvana or the record company said to do it. So, when they pressed the first twenty thousand or so CDs, albums, and cassettes, it wasn't on there."

Obviously, the first-pressing omission of "Endless, Nameless" did not affect sales of the album, because fans had no idea it was supposed to be hidden on the disc in the first place. However, the quirk did create a new collectible for record buyers who found out later they had either the valuable first edition (minus the hidden song), or a more common second pressing (containing the song). Some buyers who were aware the album had a hidden track and then couldn't find it returned their CDs to record stores, trading in the more valuable "mistake" pressing for the corrected CDs (the first pressing of the CD has a total time of 42:39, while the second pressing—with "Endless, Nameless"—cues up at 59:23). Though Weinberg did not recall mastering hidden tracks onto CDs prior to *Nevermind*, he had previously buried many sonic secrets in the run-out groove of long-play albums. "Endless, Nameless" was different in that it was an entire song and was part of Nirvana's artistic statement. The omission was noticed immediately when the band played their first copy of the album. "We popped it on," Dave Grohl told an Australian radio interviewer. "We listened to it. 'Oh, let's check to see if that track is on there.' And it wasn't there!"

The next thing Weinberg recalls is the phone ringing off the hook. "I got a heavy call from Kurt screaming, 'Where the hell is the extra song?'" "Oh fuck," he told Cobain. "Don't worry, I'll fix it right away. No problem." Kurt answered back to Weinberg, "Fix it!" It was abundantly clear to Weinberg that Cobain was in creative control of *Nevermind*. Weinberg

The band celebrates the completion of the album with a dip in a pool (during a photo shoot for promotional photos that would mimic the album cover).
(PHOTOGRAPH BY KIRK WEDDLE)

added the song back onto the album's master tape, forging a ten-minute extended gap of silence after the last officially listed song, "Something in the Way." He regrets making the mistake, but he was glad the band liked the final results when the record was fixed. He also says that "Endless, Nameless" added something to the project once it was tacked on the end. "It was a cool way to put a song on the album that maybe did not fit on it [thematically]," Weinberg says, "like a separate album of its own. In the end, it was my fault. It was hilarious that it was forgotten, but it was part of the whole scenario."

As a footnote, it is interesting that the published *Nevermind* music scores for piano and guitar also omit the song "Endless, Nameless." "It just wasn't a good guitar song for scoring," says Rita Legros of Hal Leonard Publishing. "I don't think they could score it." Ironically, the publisher had intended to include a special note to consumers to be placed at the front of the music book, but that note, too, was inadvertently omitted. The message should have read, "'Endless, Nameless' is not an appropriate song for guitar scoring." "The note just got accidentally left off," says Legros.

SPANK THRU

The concept for *Nevermind's* cover came about while Cobain and Grohl were watching a television documentary that described the underwater birthing process. "We thought that was a really neat image," Cobain said on *Nevermind: It's an Interview*. "Let's put *that* on the album cover." The band got Geffen art director Robert Fisher on the case, and he found several pictures of babies being born underwater. Unfortunately, most of those shots were considered too graphic by the label, so their second choice was a picture of a baby swimming. A photo was chosen from a stock photography agency, and mock-ups of the cover were drawn up. However, Geffen failed to come to terms with the photo agency, which wanted an exorbitant amount of money for the rights to the photo. Geffen responded by sending underwater photographer Kirk Weddle out to take shots of a four-month-old baby named Spencer Eldon submerged in a swimming pool. At the photo shoot, little Spencer was placed in a hot tub for a practice dip before the real shoot began. His mom, Renata Eldon, explained to *People* magazine how the famous album cover pose was accomplished: "We put him in the water twice, really fast, when the sun came out." The session with Spencer, the results of which would grace one of rock's most memorable album covers, was over in a flash. "It was a four-second deal," Spencer's father, Rick Eldon, told *People*. "Spencer didn't even cry." For his efforts, the youngster was paid the handsome sum of two hundred dollars. After the album climbed the charts, Spencer surely became the youngest person ever to receive a platinum record award. It proudly hangs in the youngster's bedroom.

At first the label balked at running a photo showing the baby's penis, and a mock-up was done with the penis airbrushed out. Cobain responded to this by suggesting that a sticker be placed on the album that would read, "If you're offended by this, you must be a closet pedophile." Geffen backed down and decided to go ahead with the naked-baby picture. Spencer's dad (with tongue firmly in cheek) summed up the historic place his son's image now holds in rock history. "He did what David Bowie and the Rolling Stones could never do," says Eldon. "Full frontal nudity."

The famous fishhook and dollar bill were not present at the photo shoot but were instead a Cobain afterthought. "When we got back a picture of a baby underwater," recalled Kurt for *Nevermind: It's an Interview*, "we thought it would look nice for [there to be] a fishhook with a dollar bill on it. So the image was born." To photograph the dollar, Cobain called up his friend Michael Lavine, a New York photographer who had worked with the band in the past. "They asked me to shoot the dollar, and I did it in my studio," Lavine remembers. "It was my dollar. They superimposed it over the image."

NEVERMIND/NIRVANA

The interior photos were also shot by Lavine. He had been friends with the band for several years and had gone to Evergreen State College in Olympia with Sub Pop's Bruce Pavitt. When Sub Pop wasn't using Charles Peterson for its album sleeves, it was using Lavine. He'd done several other sessions with the band, including some shots around the time of the Smart Studios recordings that, in all likelihood, would have been used for the next Sub Pop album if that record had been released. When it came time to shoot material for *Nevermind*, Cobain asked Geffen to hire Lavine. The photographer flew out to Los Angeles during the recording of the album to do some sessions.

Lavine says they rented a studio in West Hollywood and shot all day. If Cobain looks unhappy in the photos, Lavine has an explanation: "Kurt was really drunk, and he had an infection in his mouth. His gums were all infected, his lower gums. He was like, 'Oh, look at this.' You were like, 'Oh, that's all right.' He was really tired. And he drank a whole quart of Jim Beam. We shot in a studio all day, and then we walked about in the street and shot there too."

There were a few assistants on the shoot, and Lavine says the band even consented to a few clothing changes, cooperation that was not Nirvana's usual style. Afterward, Lavine says, the band selected the pho-

An underwater photo session attempted to follow the theme of the album cover. (PHOTOGRAPH BY KIRK WEDDLE)

tos to be used, and they were insistent on using the one of Cobain raising his middle finger. "They liked the blurry pictures," he says.

The back cover photo was literally a Kurt Cobain creation from start to finish. It features a rubber monkey named Chim-Chim that Kurt had owned for years. The hellish background was made by Kurt when he was in his self-described "Bohemian" photography stage, and for years it hung on his refrigerator door in Olympia. He explained for *Nevermind: It's an Interview* that it came at a time when he was "taking a bunch of weird, arty pictures. It's a collage I made many years ago. I got these pictures of beef from a supermarket poster, cut them out, and made a mountain of beef. And then I put Dante's people all over it." The collage featured not only pictures of beef and men and women burning in Dante's *Inferno*, but also shots of diseased vaginas from Cobain's own collection of medical photos. As if a hidden song buried at the end of the CD was not enough, there was a subliminal aspect to the monkey photo. "If you look real close, there is a picture of Kiss in the back standing on a slab of beef," Cobain revealed.

In July 1991, DGC prepared a press release to announce Nirvana's major-label debut. When the publicity department asked Nirvana for some biographical details, the band decided to make up a mythical history that fit the most extreme stereotype of backwoods rednecks (they'd previously created other fictitious biographies that had been issued through Sub Pop). Cooperating with the publicity department at DGC must have seemed like a trivial exercise to the band, who were confident that their new release would sell in the tens of thousands.

Filled with humorous anecdotes, in-jokes, and outright fabrications, and dripping with sarcasm, it is a classic piece of Nirvana. The band seems loose and relaxed in their own self-deprecating description of the music. In between the lies, there are a few gems of truth: "Our songs also have the standard pop format," wrote Cobain. "Verse, chorus, verse, chorus, solo, bad solo. All in all, I think we sound like the Knack and the Bay City Rollers being molested by Black Flag and Black Sabbath." Dave Grohl was quoted as saying, "Yea, I can see an inverted cross draped with plaid scarves drawn by Raymond Pettibone while he's whistling 'My Sharona.'" The band probably weren't kidding when they mentioned the Knack as an influence: one listen to the instrumental bridge on *Nevermind*'s "Territorial Pissings" confirms more than a musical nod to "My Sharona"'s introductory guitar hook (later on, Nirvana covered "My

Sharona" in concert). In a personal observation reminiscent of Groucho Marx's famous wordplay, Krist Novoselic added, "Pop is the strongest of our sensibilities, 'cause God knows we don't have any common sense."

It was when writing about Nirvana's origin that the band members really began to howl. "Nirvana's beginnings are the typical two-bored-art-students-dropping-out kind of story. Cobain, a saw blade painter specializing in Wildlife and Seascapes, met Novoselic at the Grays Harbor Institute of Northwest Crafts. Both had come from nearby Aberdeen, Washington, a small, secluded logging community seventy miles southwest of Seattle. Novoselic had a passion for gluing seashells and driftwood on burlap and, he remembers, 'I liked what Kurt was doing. I asked him what his thoughts were on a macaroni mobile piece I was working on. He suggested I glue glitter on it. That really made it!' The incident formed the basis of Nirvana's musical magic."

As always, Kurt reserved the last word for himself, as he explained the rationale behind the album and its curious title. For this one section of the bio, Cobain probably meant everything he wrote: "No one, especially people our own age, wants to address important issues. They'd rather say, 'Nevermind, forget it.' On one hand, we're not a political band—we're just some guys playing music—but we're not just another mindless band asking people to forget either. There's no rebellion in rock 'n' roll anymore. I hope underground music can influence the mainstream and shake up the kids. Maybe we can change some kid's life and stop him from becoming a welder or a sleazy lawyer. Maybe what we need is a new generation gap."

If what the world needed in 1991 was a new generation gap, Nevermind was the album to document that split. The title of the record originally came from a line in "Smells Like Teen Spirit," but Cobain's analysis—that there was a lack of political activism and a world of apathy out there—fit perfectly with the concept of a new generation responding to the mess of modern society with the apathetic sentiment of "never mind." Novoselic says that Cobain was the first one to suggest Nevermind as a potential title, but that it wasn't until the end of the recording sessions that any titles were considered. "Kurt said, 'We should just name this record Nevermind.' And I said, 'Yeah, that sounds cool.'"

"Nevermind": The word was ideal for an album title since it worked as a metaphor; it was short and easy to remember; as one word it was even grammatically incorrect and hadn't been used as a title before; and, like the names of most great albums of earlier eras, it wasn't the name of a song on the record. If the record had been titled "Smells Like Teen Spirit," that small change alone would have had major consequences for how the album was sold and remembered; that title would have seemed altogether too commercial, too obvious, and too plain dumb for Nirvana. No song on the album needed the role as title song, and none deserved to be taken out of the context of the rest of the work. Cobain thought about the title for days. He finally came to the conclusion that *Nevermind* was too good *not* to use as a title. It would be the perfect name for the album: a summation of cynicism, apathy, boredom, and anger in the nascent '90s.

SOMETHING IN THE WAY

The American Heritage Dictionary defines "nirvana" as "an ideal condition of rest, harmony, stability or joy." This condition might well have described the state of being for the members of Nirvana, had *Nevermind* never been released to the public. It is certain that it changed the lives of many people who were caught up in the hurricane-like phenomenon it wrought, and no one's life would be changed more than Kurt Cobain's. "Kurt was the kind of guy who would have been very satisfied playing in small clubs his entire life," Novoselic told a reporter for *Hit Parader*. "I knew him for a long time before Nirvana made it big. . . . As long as he could make enough to put gas in the car and buy strings for his guitar, he was content."

On August 27, 1991, the single "Smells Like Teen Spirit" went to radio, and two weeks later, on September 10, it was available as a commercial CD single with two non-album B-sides. It did not immediately chart. Though the single sold well, it did so only in pockets of the nation where an established fan base for Nirvana already existed—places like Seattle, Los Angeles, and New York, where the band had played frequently over the years. Even within Geffen's marketing plans, "Teen Spirit" wasn't meant to be the big single from the record. Instead, Geffen's promotions department had planned it as the introduction to the album, with the hit commercial single to follow. This was an established pattern used to market many records at the time. "Come As You Are" was already slated as the next single, and many at Geffen thought that "Lithium" would be the breakthrough song from the album. But this marketing plan soon was abandoned, as the album and single took on a life of their own.

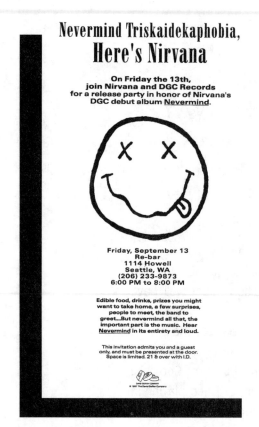

Nevermind Triskaidekaphobia, Here's Nirvana

**On Friday the 13th,
join Nirvana and DGC Records
for a release party in honor of Nirvana's
DGC debut album Nevermind.**

**Friday, September 13
Re-bar
1114 Howell
Seattle, WA
(206) 233-9873
6:00 PM to 8:00 PM**

**Edible food, drinks, prizes you might
want to take home, a few surprises,
people to meet, the band to
greet...But nevermind all that, the
important part is the music. Hear
Nevermind in its entirety and loud.**

This invitation admits you and a guest
only, and must be presented at the door.
Space is limited. 21 & over with I.D.

**The invitation to the
Nevermind record release
party at the Re-bar in
Seattle.**
(COURTESY CHARLES R.
CROSS)

Once the record took off, Geffen president Ed Rosenblatt concisely summed up the label's marketing plans to the *New York Times:* "It was just one of those 'get out of the way and duck' records."

The band held their record release party in Seattle on Friday the 13th, which would end up being a lucky day for *Nevermind*, if not for the band. The party was held at a small Seattle club called the Re-bar, and it was packed. The band members were friendly, signed autographs, and spoke highly of their new album. By the end of the evening, however, the party turned into typical Nirvana mayhem as the band members got into a battle with the club's bartender and were eventually ejected. "I remember the whole evening was drunken mania," recalls Scott Vanderpool, a DJ at the time for KXRX radio. "Everyone was completely wasted. The beer was flowing very, very freely. And then the band got kicked out."

Most people thought the band members were thrown out because they started a food fight, but Jeff Ross, who printed Nirvana's T-shirts, recalls a different reason for the conflict: "I remember them getting thrown out of the bar for bringing their own liquor in. They had some bottles of bourbon, and Krist started pouring his own drinks, and that was the reason they threw him out. Because it would have been big trouble for having liquor in there, with the liquor department and all." After the band was ejected, the Re-bar party continued without them. The band members milled around outside the club for a short while and then retreated to Ross's loft, where they continued to celebrate. After fire extinguishers were let off and everyone got kicked out of the loft (two ejections in one night!), the crew headed off for a third and final party stop at Susie Tennant's house. All in all, it would be one of the most celebratory nights in Nirvana's history.

On September 24, 1991, the *Nevermind* album was released. It entered inauspiciously at Number 144 on the *Billboard* charts. The predictions on the part of the band were modest. Kurt told *Billboard* maga-zine, "I expected our core audience to buy our record within the first cou-ple of weeks and then the sales would decline after that. But after I real-ized that we were on MTV, I suspected we would sell a lot more." In fact, the album's initial sales never did decline, but rather continued to rise steadily for almost a year. Six months after it was released, the album was selling four times as many copies in a week as it had during the first week it was out.

In *Nevermind: It's an Interview*, the band tried to explain their suc-cess: "It was sort of an organic thing. There wasn't any massive hype," Grohl said. Bass player Novoselic was more to the point: "Whatever hap-pened was surely out of our control." Cobain pointed out that the record took off without a big-budget advertising campaign: "There was definitely no big million-dollar investment in promotion behind this record at all."

Cobain wasn't exaggerating: the promotional efforts were modest by any standard. Though Geffen had high hopes for the album, they pur-chased only a few ads for it in selected alternative publications. The press promotion was low key by the standards of a major label. "When we got advance cassettes (we didn't even do CDs then), I did a selected mailing to maybe three hundred critics," remembers Lisa Gladfelter-Bell, the Geffen publicist assigned to *Nevermind*. "I targeted publications like *Rolling Stone* and *Spin*, with long lead times that were geared towards music, and then the Seattle area magazines like *The Rocket*. Included in that first mailing were about twenty-five to thirty-five of the major top-circulation dailies. I remember, from day one, getting good feedback. And this was really silly, but my thought at the time was, 'This band isn't even going to sell an album.' I thought that because critics liked it so much, it wouldn't sell."

Critics don't buy albums, and the list of critical favorites that have died at the sales counter is long and storied. But the initial critical response surprised Gladfelter-Bell and encouraged the company to con-sider upping the album's original press run. "I had even hard-core critics, who never will call you back, calling and raving about it—everyone from *Circus* to people who I could never get on the phone," she says. "The response to it was really great, right away." Gladfelter-Bell says the initial run of the CD was planned for 25,000 copies, but as response from press and radio poured in, that figure was upped to 46,251 in the United States and 35,000 in the U.K. (*Bleach* had been big in England).

The response within the walls of the Geffen office was also positive. Even before the album was released, it became the favorite record of the mostly young staff at the label. "Everyone in the company loved the record," remembers Gladfelter-Bell. Though the young Geffen staffers liked the record, no one at the label proposed spending a lot of money to launch it. "The plan was to do the slow grassroots thing, thinking it would build," says Gladfelter-Bell. Other than the early promo cassettes, and the humorous bios penned by the band, there were only a few promotional items issued. One was a mobile that was created for record stores, which featured a cut-out image of the baby chasing the dollar bill. There were posters of the album cover, a T-shirt with the band's name and logo, and a color postcard, but all these things were standard for any release. "We weren't skimping or anything," Gladfelter-Bell explains, "but that was about it. It was typical at the time. A lot of bands ended up doing nothing on Geffen, so we always started slow."

The only other promotional item, Gladfelter-Bell says, was a T-shirt that was made up in infant sizes: "Because the baby was on the front of the record, they made maybe fifty or a hundred of these baby shirts. They were the cutest things, little infant-sized T-shirts that said 'Nirvana, *Nevermind'* on them. I think I was given about ten, and I gave them to the people I knew who had kids." No one in the company bothered to give the band any of the infant-sized shirts.

Gladfelter-Bell then began the process of setting up interviews for the group. The band made it clear to their label that they were willing and eager to talk to any- and everyone who wanted to speak with them. They did about three dozen interviews during the months of September and October, but by far the majority of these were with newspapers and radio in Seattle—interest from the other parts of the nation was slow to develop until the single took off. "We worked hard," Novoselic says of the many interviews the band did. "We gave it everything."

Most interviewers who encountered Nirvana found the band full of optimism and excitement. "There was an innocence," says Damon Stewart, who interviewed the band for Seattle radio station KISW during September. "Those guys were excited just to have their music on the radio, and they knew what it meant to go on the radio and talk about it. They wanted to turn other people on to the kind of music they liked and were listening to." Stewart, who had interviewed the band several times in

The official promo photo issued with *Nevermind*, shot by Chris Cuffaro. (PHOTOGRAPH COURTESY EXPERIENCE MUSIC PROJECT)

the previous years, says he was still shocked at how excited they were simply about being interviewed. "They were more happy about you wanting to do an interview with them than they were to actually do the interview itself. They were flattered." That sense of flattery would last for only a few weeks, as the group soon became weary of all the press attention, but initially they approached interviews like eager new employees in a corporate cog. Novoselic explained to *The Rocket* that interviews were just "something you gotta do if you wanna get promotion."

The weeks before the record was released were in many ways the apex of Nirvana's happiness during their entire career. In conversations with both friends and the press, they were exuberant. Cobain even found time to do a phone interview with Patrick MacDonald from the *Seattle Times*, the largest newspaper in Washington and a far cry from the fanzines that were his usual preference for interviews. Even at this point, filled with what MacDonald calls a "positively boyish zeal," Cobain wasn't above a little mischief: "He tried to sell me this story about how he'd bought an inflatable love doll and he'd cut the hands and feet and put a slit up the back and he'd climbed inside," MacDonald remembers. "I knew while he was telling me this that he wanted me to print it, but I also knew it was a lie. I went back and forth, but I didn't print it. I thought it was funny that he wanted to play."

Interviews would soon become a tiresome requirement of their job, but during September 1991, the band members wanted to "play" with reporters as much as they could. Kurt told the Seattle fanzine *Hype* that their label had provided them with a tour van that was complete with "a foot massager, a water pick, and a humidifier. We're going to be shooting up aloe vera and warm milk speedballs." With Seattle's *The Rocket* the band was more serious, complaining to Jennifer Boddy that they were already getting tired of interviews. "We're just now coming into doing so many interviews that we're becoming exhausted by it," Cobain explained. "I mean, every waking day of my life is Nirvana now. Phone interviews and just constantly being tooled around." Novoselic, always the optimist, found joy even in being the center of attention: "But at least we can get stoned and stuff," he said. "We try to make the best of it. Try to wreck some guy's car, throw pizza at each other, kooky, zany things, you know. Squirting flowers, hand buzzers . . ."

As the single began to take off, the requests for interviews began to grow. But despite the airplay, the album did not initially garner an inordinate number of rave reviews; *Rolling Stone* gave the release only three of five possible stars. *Nevermind* being a debut album, many newspapers and magazines at first ignored it altogether. Three months later, print media would be scrambling to cover the phenomenon of the album's success, but at that point they were writing more about Kurt Cobain than the record.

However, the reviews that did appear were generally positive. *The Rocket* called it a milestone album within the Northwest music scene. "It was the kind of music that you fell in love with," the review read. "Nirvana is the best band in the world at singing 'yea, yay, yah, yeahayea.'" In *Rolling Stone* Ira Robbins wrote, "If Nirvana isn't onto anything altogether new, *Nevermind* does possess the songs, character and confident spirit to be much more than a reformulation of college radio's high octave hits." *Spin* compared the band to their forebears: "Nirvana's music sounds like R.E.M. married to Sonic Youth, while having an affair with the Germs."

England's *Melody Maker* referred to Nirvana as "one of the most visceral, intense and beautiful bands on the face of the planet," while America's *Billboard* provided a more detached perspective for the disc they dubbed a "hard-rocking sludgeorama." In a comment directed more toward radio programmers and retailers than consumers, the *Billboard* reviewer remarked, "Power trio crunches brutally, but never at the expense of hooks that should snag modern rockers. Lead-off track 'Smells Like Teen Spirit,' 'Come As You Are,' 'Breed,' and 'Stay Away' all have enough fever to snare target audiences."

Not all of the reviews were positive. Though *Rolling Stone*'s review was mostly kind, the three-stars rating—assigned, as in all *Rolling Stone* reviews, by the editors, not the writer—was faint praise. Some of the most damning criticism the record received came from the *Boston Globe*'s Steve Morse, who wrote, "Most of *Nevermind* is packed with generic punk-pop that's been done better by countless acts from Iggy Pop to the Red Hot Chili Peppers. And because the band has little or nothing to say, settling for moronic ramblings by singer-lyricist Cobain, who has an idiotic tendency to sound like the Rod McKuen of hard rock—that is, when he's not sounding like some dunderhead down at the Fake Rebellion Cafe. . . ." The band might have enjoyed that review, if only because of the reference to Rod McKuen, whom they'd mentioned in one of their fake biographies.

While most print media embraced *Nevermind*, radio proved a harder nut to crack. While popular mythology has suggested that *Nevermind* was a hit from the moment it came out and that "Teen Spirit" was an anthem the day it was released, the truth is that the record was slow to take off. And though the album would eventually hit the top of the charts, the "Teen Spirit" single only made it as high as Number 6 on the *Billboard* charts. "It began as a battle," recalls Susie Tennant, the DGC employee responsible for working the record in its most friendly market, Northwest radio. "And there were all the guys I faced [in] rock radio who told me, 'We can't play it, because we can't hear what he's saying.' In Seattle, all three rock stations were really supportive, but that was in Seattle only. Trying to work the rest of the Northwest wasn't easy."

The record didn't initially chart higher, says Novoselic, because "it *couldn't*. That was the climate the record came into." At the time, most rock radio stations weren't supporting alternative rock.

But once again, *Nevermind* benefited from perfect timing. Just a few short weeks before "Smells Like Teen Spirit" was sent to radio, a new radio station and format debuted in Seattle with station 107.7 FM, named The End. While Seattle had previously had three alternative-rock stations (KZAM, KJET, and KYYX), all three had gone off the air, leaving only the college station KCMU to play anything not commercial. And though The End was tailor-made for Nirvana (and eventually the band's music would become the cornerstone of the alternative format nationwide), even this station didn't jump all over the single immediately. Essentially, The End (along with other stations in the Seattle market) played "Smells Like Teen Spirit" only at night, thinking that it would turn off listeners during the day.

"At first, I can remember putting the single into nighttime rotation only," recalls Marco Collins, music director of The End. "We had done what's called 'day parting' of the song because we thought the song was a little too aggressive for the daytime. And then watching the reaction over the next three weeks was pretty insane. It built and built and built. We got great phones, but because we live in a market that is so localized, and musicians here had the support of the local community, we really felt that we were on to something with the band here in Seattle, but we didn't think of it as being part of a national vibe."

That nighttime-only policy would soon change, as The End, and Seattle's other stations, started getting such "great phones" requesting Nirvana during the day that they could no longer ignore the song. They began to play the single at all hours, and, eventually, to pick up the other

NEVERMIND/NIRVANA

tracks from the album. In the month that passed between the release of the single and the album's release, "Smells Like Teen Spirit" had become a phenomenon in the Seattle market. It had yet to take off in the rest of the nation.

When the album was finally released, it sold so fast in Seattle that it was temporarily unavailable; that shortfall seemed to turn even more fans to the radio with requests. Though the sales statistics are hard to pin down at this point, Geffen employees confirm that about half of the initial run of forty-six thousand went to the Northwest, where it sold like hot cakes. "I remember when the record first came out, and it sold out and wasn't available, that's when we had tons of kids calling us up bugging us because they couldn't find it," Collins recalls. "And Geffen was like, 'We had no idea.' From what I understand, every single other album was put on hold so they could make more CDs of *Nevermind*." Tower Records' Bob Zimmerman confirms the shortage of records: "There was a seven- to ten-day period where just about everybody in Seattle was out of it and it was impossible to get."

Even people who couldn't buy the album soon became fans. Radio programmers were shocked when their research indicated that people across the demographic spectrum—irrespective of age and gender— were responding positively to "Smells Like Teen Spirit." "The research was through the roof, like nothing we'd ever seen," says Collins. "For something that aggressive to be researched, we're talking about playing this track through a phone line, with fifteen-second clips, and it's still reacting with these people who were hearing it. Try to imagine what it would sound like to hear 'Teen Spirit' for the first time through a phone line, and imagine hearing only a fifteen-second clip. How do you convey that energy over a phone line? But it did. That's when it started heating up, and we realized that this was going to be *much* bigger than we initially thought."

It got bigger, and then bigger still. Though Collins says his station wanted to play other tracks from the CD, there were so many requests for "Teen Spirit" that the station could not ignore them. "We couldn't get rid of that song," he says. "We wanted to dabble in the album, but 'Teen Spirit' wouldn't go away. The height of it all was in October, November, and December. It was being played close to thirty-two hits a week. It was our most-played record for three or four months." Collins did a daily people's-choice countdown titled "The Top Ten at Ten," and he says "Smells Like Teen Spirit" so dominated the playlist that it was the top choice of listeners for over three months.

The response of listeners to The End was being repeated at other stations in Seattle, and, eventually, across the nation. DJ Scott Vanderpool says that even his station, KXRX, which usually played classic rock, began to spin the single. "We were hitting it once every three hours at the height," he remembers, "and that's a lot for radio. I was jumping up and down about it. It was my just deserts, as in some way I felt like I had been working for this for a long time." Vanderpool cites Nirvana as one of the reasons that KXRX eventually went off the air—because they couldn't find an easy way to work alternative rock into their classic format. "Nirvana totally changed rock radio," he says.

SCHOOL

For a band led by a man who hated high school, it would be the ultimate irony that a video set in a Hollywood version of a high-school gym would change his band's career. If there was one single element that shifted the success of *Nevermind* from a hit record to a phenomenon, it was the video for "Smells Like Teen Spirit." Though Cobain would grow to regret having made the video—he would eventually perform the song in concert in a slowed-down, lounge-style parody or refuse to sing it at all—even he would cite the video clip as the defining element that pushed sales of the album above the gold-record level and into the multiplatinum stratosphere.

When journalist Paddy Chng asked Cobain in April 1992 whether MTV was the "one thing that broke Nirvana," Cobain replied, "Definitely." In this surprising interview, he went on to compliment the staff at MTV and discuss how he'd been impressed with their commitment to new music—words he would later contradict. "They are really into our music and other underground bands and are trying to break these bands too," he said of MTV's executives.

It would be presumptuous to suggest that the video alone "broke" Nirvana, because even before the clip started getting airplay on MTV, the record was a hit. Long before MTV came into the picture, several circumstances came together to make *Nevermind* a successful album. Among them were the hard work the band had put in by touring for years; their groundbreaking work on *Bleach* and their other Sub Pop records; clever T-shirts that helped establish the band's identity long before the record reached a wide audience; the wide circulation of the Smart Studio "demos"; and the fact that Nirvana already boasted a cadre of believers within the music industry. This "Nirvana army," if you will, consisted of supporters from diverse fields—from T-shirt maker Jeff Ross to DGC's Susie Tennant to John Troutman, who was employed by another label—all of whom felt like Nirvana's success was *their* success. By the time *Nevermind* was released, Nirvana had their own army of salespeople in all walks of the industry; this groundwork helped ensure that the album would get an extra sales boost. Debating what "broke" the album ignores the obvious artistic achievement of the album: even if it had sold only a single copy, *Nevermind* would still rank as one of the greatest albums of the '90s, if only because of the artistic high water mark it represented. But that is something to be considered apart from commercial concerns.

Though MTV clearly wasn't the single factor that "broke" the album, it was the one element that turned a "hit" into a "crossover," at least for commercial purposes. Nirvana got lucky because one member of the Nirvana army was Amy Finnerty, who had infiltrated MTV and had a job there as a programmer. She pushed for the video and the band, and though she met with resistance, she fought until the clip got on the air. As with sales of the single and airplay on the radio, things began slowly at MTV. The video had its world premiere on the network, but only within the confines of the specialty show "120 Minutes," which in the fall of 1991 was not one of the channel's most watched programs.

The video clip had been filmed in Culver City, California, on August 17, 1991. It was filmed at GMT Studios—about ten miles away from where the album had been recorded at Sound City—on stage number six, with the shoot beginning at noon and lasting the entire day. The video was directed by Sam Bayer, and from the start the members of Nirvana were in conflict with him over the artistic vision for the clip. Bayer's concept was to show a school assembly in the gym, but the band's idea, as Dave Grohl told Michael Azerrad, leaned more toward "a pep rally from hell." The Ramones' "Rock 'n' Roll High School" was clearly an influence on both the director and the band.

But first, an audience of extras had to be recruited. "We'd done a contest on a college radio station to get people down there, and it was mostly real hipster kids," remembers Gladfelter-Bell. "The kids had to go outside between the takes because there was fire being used in the video that was in the studio and those were the rules. There were also certain takes they couldn't be on." Not only were the extras (listeners of station KXLU) forced to stand outside through numerous takes on an extremely hot day, but the small budget of thirty-three thousand dollars hadn't covered catering for them. "There were just drinks like Coke for them and nothing to eat," Gladfelter-Bell says.

Cobain clashed with Bayer over the singer's insistence that the director allow the kids to come down from the bleachers to mosh in front of the band. According to Michael Azzerad, Bayer told the throng of kids, "Nobody knock anything over until I tell you, because I want to get good close-up shots of it." But by the end of the day—after sitting through take after take and being forced to stand outside in the heat during many of the shoots—the kids began to resemble the crowd at an actual Nirvana concert. They weren't interested in following any rules. "Once the kids came out dancing they just said 'Fuck you,' because they were so tired of his shit throughout the day," Cobain told Azerrad.

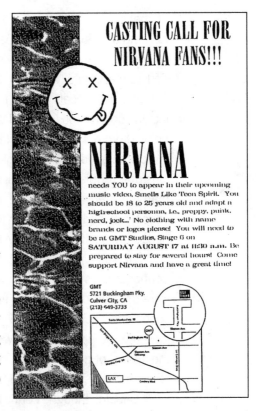

The ad that solicited extras for the "Smells Like Teen Spirit" video.

Even after the video was filmed, conflicts between Cobain and director Bayer continued in the editing process. "I came up with the idea for the 'Smells Like Teen Spirit' video, but the director had different ideas, and what emerged wasn't what I had in mind," Cobain later told Paddy Chng. "I had to go into the editing room in the last days of post-production to salvage whatever I could, like inserting certain scenes which the director had left out, to salvage it and make it tolerable. It was our mistake to go in with a commercial director." One of the scenes Cobain salvaged was the shot before the end, the close-up of his own face. It would provide the perfect ending to the video because it would connect a personality to the song. Though this one edit would help launch the single and propel the album up the charts, it also ultimately increased Cobain's fame.

Despite all the conflict, the resulting video is considered by many to be a masterpiece of the promotional video genre. It combines the power of the song's shifting chords with the style of quick editing that had become the standard for music video clips. It was aesthetically and musically a punk rebellion. The visually disturbing images were perfectly married to the carefully crafted arrangement of the song. Cobain's ambiguous, slurring vocals about feeling "stupid and contagious" created an instant connection with MTV's audience. As Michael Azerrad correctly pointed out, it had "all the classic elements of video: pretty girls in revealing clothes, kids dancing the latest dance and flaunting the latest fashions, the requisite dry ice fog, guys with long hair playing guitars." Other than the pretty girls and the dry-ice, it had nothing that a typical Nirvana concert in early 1991 didn't sport. And if a little Hollywood gloss was needed to sell the song to MTV, the band acquiesced.

"It was a great move on the part of Nirvana to do that video," notes Soundgarden's Kim Thayil. "They were dressed just like kids that age were dressed because they *were* kids that age. It was brilliant to use high school kids. It addressed who they were playing for. It said, 'There you guys are, here we are, and we're *you*.'" Thayil's point succinctly sums up the appeal of not only the video, but the single, the album, and the band: Nirvana were still not above their audience; they remained at one with it.

Cobain, though, continued to struggle with the idea of doing any video, and in interviews he went back and forth on whether the video was a good or a bad idea. Several times he found himself defending the very idea of doing a video in the first place when he spoke with journalists, noting that "even the Ramones have made a movie." He was defensive about the concept, even when he was being prodded about it. Still, in describing the video to Patrick MacDonald on the day of the album's release, Cobain would sound surprisingly practical: "We really don't have much of an image, so it's fine with us if someone exaggerates a bit."

After its debut on "120 Minutes," the video—like the radio single before it—was sent to nighttime rotation, because MTV's programmers shared radio's concerns about the aggressive nature of the song. But the video was selected as a "Buzz Bin" clip on October 14, three weeks after the release of the album. MTV had found, as had radio, that both research and viewer response were overwhelmingly positive. As MTV executive Abbey Konowich explained to *Billboard,* "It virtually exploded. It had all those elements to be cutting-edge, but at the same time had mass appeal." MTV kept the clip as its "Buzz Bin" selection for nine weeks,

until the middle of December. By that point, the video clip, the single, and the album were runaway hits.

Then *Nevermind* did an amazing thing: the album *and* single started to cross over, from MTV to commercial radio, from college radio to Top 40, from Top 40 to album-oriented rock radio. It became something extremely rare in the music industry: a cross-format phenomenon, hitting all the current major rock categories including modern rock, hard rock, album rock, and college radio.

By early December 1991, Cobain was telling interviewers that the success of the record was "frightening." Sounding quite unlike most musicians with a hit record, he frankly admitted that the success "scared" him. As the band played Europe in late November and early December, the group drew crowds who were less Nirvana fans than "Smells Like Teen Spirit" fans. While doing a video shoot in Amsterdam, the band

Nirvana at their New York City Tower Records' in-store.
(PHOTOGRAPH BY MAX GOLDSTEIN)

developed a new approach to dealing with the tedium of performing the song day in and day out. Without making any attempt to mask the fact that they were pretending to play over an instrumental soundtrack tape, Cobain sang the song an entire octave lower, in a '60s cocktail lounge singer's voice. The contrast between his smooth, Valium-sounding delivery and the lyrics was quite amusing to those who got the joke. He also changed the opening lines to "Load up on drugs and kill your friends." As the song built to a climax, Novoselic and Grohl flailed around wildly, smiling and making no attempt to play their instruments. Unbelievably, the self-parody of this performance was lost on the fanatical kids dancing in front of the stage, who slam-danced into each other with reckless abandon.

A few weeks later when Nirvana performed live on a British television show, the band began to play the now familiar opening riffs of "Smells Like Teen Spirit," only to let the song fall apart before the vocals began. A snickering Krist Novoselic walked up to the microphone, as Cobain turned to check his amp, and informed the shocked audience, "We're going to skip that one."

TERRITORIAL PISSINGS

By November 1991, Nirvana were not only bearing the cross of "Smells Like Teen Spirit," a song that was far more popular than they ever could have imagined any single they would produce could be; they were also saddled with what Seattleites began to call "the G-word." Virtually no media report—in newspapers, television, or on radio—in the fall of 1991 failed to describe Nirvana as a "grunge band." "Grunge" became the easy catchall phrase to describe what was new and special about Nirvana. And for the band, the "grunge" moniker became the linchpin of all they hated about success, fame, and overexposure.

Never mind that Nirvana were not technically a "grunge" band at all. "Grunge" was locally defined—by members of Seattle bands and those in the Northwest music press—as distorted, tuned-down, riff-heavy rock music that used feedback and ponderous bass lines to carry the melody.

To purists, the best examples of bands that "correctly" can be called "grunge" are: Blood Circus (who virtually defined the genre); Tad (their heaviness was not just because of Tad Doyle's girth!); the Fluid (a Sub Pop band that wasn't even from Seattle); and Mudhoney (who began as a "grunge" band with songs like "Touch Me, I'm Sick," but evolved, if you will, into more of a garage-rock band). "The phenomenon of 'grunge' was a culmination of twenty years of punk rock," notes critic Grant Alden. Nirvana, with pop sensibilities and influences that were equal parts Sonic Youth and Cheap Trick, were not playing the same game. Early in their career, when Nirvana played on bills with the Fluid and Blood Circus, the contrast was notable, and the sound of Nirvana was lightweight in com-

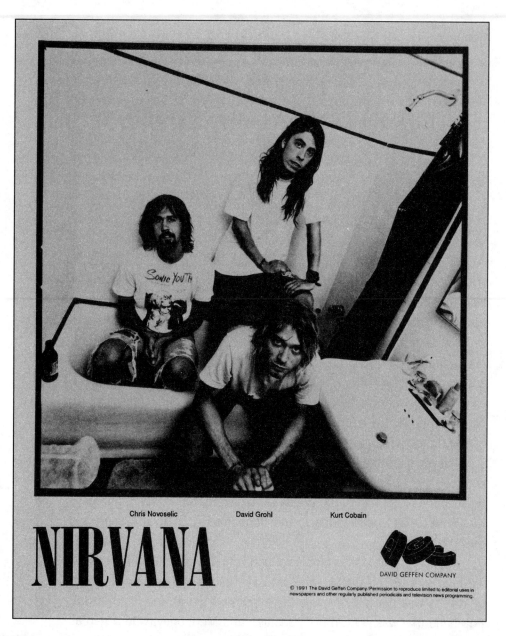

Chris Novoselic   David Grohl   Kurt Cobain

NIRVANA

DAVID GEFFEN COMPANY

© 1991 The David Geffen Company/Permission to reproduce limited to editorial uses in newspapers and other regularly published periodicals and television news programming.

The second official Geffen promo photo from *Nevermind*, shot by Chris Cuffaro.
(PHOTOGRAPH COURTESY EXPERIENCE MUSIC PROJECT)

parison. The closest the group ever came to "grunge" was the sound of *Bleach*, and that probably had more to do with the production style of Jack Endino than it did with Nirvana's songs or playing. But accuracy has never been the hallmark of the press, and when a few U.K. journalists began to take holidays to Seattle in the summer of 1989 and christen what they heard "the grunge scene," Nirvana was listed right next to Blood Circus as purveyors of this new sound.

Nirvana hated the term. Any time a television reporter in the U.S. got anywhere near the band in the fall of 1991, the first question asked of the band was always about "grunge." It was even worse in Europe, where it seemed that "grunge" was all that the interviewers wanted to discuss. "Grunge" had become bigger than the band themselves. When the Dutch magazine *OOR* asked Dave Grohl to list his frustrations, the first thing he cited was the labeling. "Suddenly all kinds of labels appeared, 'alternative music,' 'grunge,'" he said. "But sometimes, you think to yourself, 'Fuck, in the end, isn't it all music?'"

Even self-proclaimed "pop geek" Butch Vig says that Nirvana was neither the first "grunge" band nor the defining one, and though he has since been saddled with the "grunge" label himself, he disputes that the term accurately describes *Nevermind*. "I remember when *Nevermind* was just starting to take off," he recalls. "I was talking about the whole 'grunge' phenomenon with a friend in L.A. when 'Helter Skelter' came on the juke-box. I said, 'Here's the first grunge song, listen to it!' It sounded just amazing, you know, the guitar and McCartney's voice. 'Grunge' wasn't really anything new. I didn't invent grunge. And Seattle didn't invent it either." The roots of distorted, bass-heavy rock music go back a lot farther than the Beatles. But "grunge" may have begun in the Northwest, since this style can be best applied to the "Louie, Louie"–era bands the Sonics and the Kingsmen.

Whether "grunge" was an apt description of Nirvana's music didn't matter much late in the fall of 1991, but the tag did help sell the album to the masses. "Grunge" basically became a marketing term that soon encompassed fashion (Perry Ellis flannel shirts); novelty products (a "grunge" air-freshener; "grunge" hair gel); and even a CD of easy-listening music (titled *Grunge Lite*). There is no denying that the "grunge" label helped *Nevermind* to reach out and draw in buyers from America's heartland who had no familiarity with what a Blood Circus song might sound like.

For the angst-ridden generation of kids who had been searching for music they could claim as their own, *Nevermind* was a milestone album. In many ways it was their "chosen" record, an album that became as

much a part of the journey from adolescence to adulthood as Clearasil, Nintendo 64, or nose piercings. But more than just a rite of passage—which is the role a lightweight pop song would have—this album was a rallying cry, a single explosion of anger that spoke for the anger of millions. Only a record as emotional and as honest as *Nevermind* could have played this role.

In the years preceding *Nevermind*'s release, the most successful genre of music had been big-hair metal, and it was no small irony that Nirvana followed Warrant into Sound City Studios. By the time *Nevermind* was finished, Warrant's career was over. But even though metal bands like Warrant and Guns N' Roses sold millions of albums, their records never served as "generational glue" in the manner that *Nevermind* did. The social phenomenon that followed *Nevermind* brought to mind the pivotal works *Led Zeppelin I*, the Beatles' *Revolver*, the Beach Boys' *Pet Sounds*, and the Sex Pistols' *Never Mind the Bollocks*—albums that, each in its own way, captured a single movement in the collective pop-culture consciousness. For one brief moment in the fall of 1991, an entire generation of youths had gathered to listen to one piece of music by one band.

Though it began in the U.S. and the U.K., it soon went worldwide. When Jack Endino toured Europe with his band, Skinyard, in the fall of 1991, he was shocked to hear his old friends on every radio he passed. "By the time our tour got to Europe," Endino recalls, "which I think was October, the whole thing had started to explode. We started hearing 'Smells Like Teen Spirit' everywhere we went. Literally. People's houses, radio stations, record stores. We'd meet up with someone and they'd have a tape of it. People were passing tapes of the album around.

"We played a show in Bergen, Norway, which is miles away from anywhere. It's out on the coast, and you have to take a train to get there because there are no roads. And when we got there, they had a tape of the album that they were playing on the PA system of the club. The record hadn't been released in Norway yet or anywhere in Scandinavia. And it was everywhere. We began to almost feel hunted by it."

By November 1991, *Nevermind* was one of the top five albums in sales at such prominent chains as National Record Mart, Specs, Flip Side, Rose Records, Title Wave, and Music Plus. Musicland, a thousand-store chain at the time, had *Nevermind* selling in its number-eight spot. *Billboard* did a story on the success of the record, and Nirvana co-

By the time of this Seattle photo session, the "grunge" hype was taking its toll on the band.
(PHOTOGRAPH BY CHARLES PETERSON/RETNA)

manager John Silva repeated the prevailing Geffen sentiment: "The watchword for all of this has been, 'Get out of the way.'" Danny Goldberg, the other principal in Gold Mountain, told *Billboard* pretty much the same thing: "They've tapped into a wave of interest on the part of an audience seeking a departure from the status quo of rock bands."

In *Billboard,* fans could chart the album's amazing climb. In one week, *Nevermind* rose from Number 144 to 109. It quickly jumped to 65 . . . and then to 35, hovering in the Top 10 during the 1991 holiday season.

No one at Geffen had been prepared for this level of success, which was part of the reason why the label had shortages of CDs early on. Before the album was released, the band's A&R representative, Gary Gersh, explained the label's expectations to Vig: "They've got a hard-core cult following," Vig recalls him saying. "I think we'll sell about 150,000 or 200,000 on this. And maybe we'll have a gold record." As it was, the album went platinum—marking one million copies sold—on November 29, 1991, just two months after its release, and it was double-platinum by the first week of January.

By the last week of December 1991, weekly sales of the record reached yet another plateau. SoundScan figures show it sold an amazing 373,250 copies in that one week. According to Bob Zimmerman of Tower Records, many of those sales can be credited to kids returning unwanted Christmas gifts. "We saw so many kids come in with whatever CD their parents had bought for them that holiday—many were Michael Jackson— and they were exchanging them all for *Nevermind*," says Zimmerman. "There were just legions of kids returning the music their parents had given them and buying *Nevermind* instead."

One thing that benefited *Nevermind* greatly was SoundScan itself, the measuring device that electronically tracks point-of-sale business. *Billboard*—the dominant music trade publication—adopted the SoundScan method for determining record sales charts in January 1991. Previously, albums had charted based on what record store employees reported, a process that was not always accurate and was susceptible to label lobbying. SoundScan was a more scientific process in that it tallied actual sales. From its inception it proved that the previous charts had inaccurately favored veteran acts and were not reflecting enough sales of new talent and genres. Though rap and country gained market shares with the advent of SoundScan, so did alternative rock.

Nevermind can be thought of as the first rock record that was a "SoundScan surprise," as those in the industry would call it. If the old system of chart reporting had still been in place when *Nevermind* was released, it is doubtful the album would have scored so high, considering that the band was unknown to many in the industry and did not benefit from a huge promotional push. But by the end of 1991, even those who had never before heard of Nirvana were taking notice after seeing the group's name atop industry sales charts.

Vig remembers talking with John Silva after the album was in the *Billboard* Top 10, at the first of the year. "I asked him, 'Any chance it's going Number 1?' He said, 'Not a chance.'" Vig smiles when he adds, "It went to Number 1 the next week." That was the week of January 11, 1992, the day Nirvana made their first appearance on *Saturday Night Live*. Not only had Nirvana hit the top of charts only three months after *Nevermind* had been released, they had taken the top slot away from superstar Michael Jackson. It was, as Novoselic notes, "a coup. It was a total coup."

The coup would be not simply symbolic, as Vig notes that all the major labels "started scrambling to sign anything that had a flannel shirt and a distorted guitar." *Nevermind* would stay in one of the top three spots on the *Billboard* charts until April.

ON A PLAIN

When it came time to analyze why *Nevermind* was such a success, there were almost as many pundits as there were copies of the album in print. Few commentators were able to improve upon Soundgarden's Kim Thayil's comment that the key was the band's relationship with their audience: "There you guys are, here we are, and we're *you*." Much was made in the media about how the album captured "the angst of a generation." But the sales of *Nevermind* were so high that it clearly wasn't just teenagers needing an angst fix who bought the record. *Nevermind* was a true crossover album in every sense of the word; because it appealed to so many different ages, genders, and nationalities of people, it was one of the few albums of the '90s that found its way into almost every record collection. And despite the fact that the album sold over ten million copies, it has had staying power and has remained a staple of alternative radio.

Putting aside all of the sociological mass-media hype, the only plausible theory for *Nevermind*'s amazing success, according to Butch Vig, was the music itself. "A lot of kids were looking for something that felt more real and had more passion," he says. "And *Nevermind* definitely had it, certainly compared to a lot of the really slick pop stuff that was on the charts at the time, like C & C Music Factory or Madonna. Kids were tired of being force fed music that was polished and overproduced. For a punk record, *Nevermind* had a certain degree of polish. The performances were really focused and tight, but there was a ton of passion on it. They wrote killer songs. And at the time, there wasn't a whole lot of music coming out that had that kind of angst and passion. It was just one

From a photo session in Seattle.
(PHOTOGRAPH BY CHARLES PETERSON/RETNA)

134

of these things, where they happened to have the right thing at the right time."

Even Novoselic says that timing had a lot to do with the success of *Nevermind*. "A lot of it was being in the right place at the right time. There were bands that opened doors for us, like Jane's Addiction and Faith No More, like Sonic Youth and Dinosaur Jr., who made beautiful records, and . . . still [do]," he says.

The "right place, right time" theory is echoed by many in the industry, but no analysis is complete without noting that the record's success marked a great shift in the taste of record buyers. According to Andy Wallace, whose mixes were calculated to make the songs jump out of car radios everywhere, "*Nevermind* represented a major turning point in the style of music. It was a powerhouse album that got everyone to listen with new ears." Howie Weinberg remembers thinking at the time, "It's a nice alternative record. It might get some airplay. But sometimes amazing things just happen by circumstance."

Superstar drummer Jim Keltner, known for his session work and for playing with John Lennon, was neither the first nor the last to draw a comparison between Kurt Cobain and Lennon. "Kurt really reminded me a lot of John in his writing, singing, and guitar playing," Keltner says. "More attitude than technique, but he had incredibly strong rhythm and a great solo sense. Nirvana's *Nevermind* album is as good as anything ever produced in rock 'n' roll. It was talking to me. I'd finally heard a new band speaking to me from the past, present, and future."

Keltner's point is seconded by many who note that *Nevermind* brought music a step forward while at the same time reminding listeners of the past. Seven years after it was recorded, it doesn't sound significantly dated. "The mainstream is always searching for something new," remarks Tom Walker, owner/operator of a small-market radio chain called Midwest Management. "Look back at the Beatles breaking out from England, and in the late '70s, with Blondie and the Talking Heads coming out of New York. They all took some of the sounds and styles before them and turned them into something new." Walker suggests the music of *Nevermind* provided rock music with long-overdue recycling.

Certainly some of that recycling came from Northwest roots and probably developed from the records that Cobain and Novoselic had found in second-hand stores in Aberdeen. Nirvana recycled the original

Northwest sound of the Sonics, Wailers, and Kingsmen—remember, those bands were sticking pencils into speakers to create more distortion—but they moved that raw sound ahead thirty years at the same time. "Here in the Northwest," says the *Seattle Times'* Patrick MacDonald, "we had one of the *first* important rock 'n' roll records in 'Louie, Louie,' and also the *last* important rock record in 'Smells Like Teen Spirit.' It's the last great rock 'n' roll record I know of. They were two brackets on the history of rock right there. 'Teen Spirit,' and the album too, took the whole history of rock 'n' roll and moved it forward. It took all the traditions of rock 'n' roll, without being corny and without exploiting it. One of the great things about Kurt was his open mind about all music. He wasn't the type to say, 'I hate this, I hate that.' It's the past but it's also the future."

Nirvana certainly weren't unique in the way they mixed the rock stylings of the past with new twists. The fusion of punk and pop had been done numerous times before by the likes of Pere Ubu, Patti Smith, the Velvet Underground, and dozens of other bands in the ten years between the birth of punk and the success of Nirvana. Yet Cobain wasn't a fanatical student of rock history—instead he looked to the second wave of New York art bands, like his often-mentioned Sonic Youth, for inspiration. If Cobain had tried to emulate the first wave of post-punk bands, Nirvana's music might have been more derivative, or he might have been discouraged. Part of Cobain's genius came from his naïveté: he didn't know he was treading familiar turf, so he wasn't afraid to try a style of music that many in rock thought was tapped out. And he benefited greatly by the fact that the music world was long overdue for a rock group that could modernize early punk.

What made *Nevermind* an important record, though, wasn't the fact that it marked the evolution of a trend—*some* post-punk band was destined to take punk back into the mainstream, and, even as Nirvana achieved that goal, critics were surprised the feat hadn't been done by the Replacements or Hüsker Dü. Instead, what made *Nevermind* a great album was the way Cobain, Novoselic, Grohl, and Vig managed to create music that conveyed so much emotion. The songs themselves—their undeniable lyric power and catchy melodies paired with the impassioned playing of the band—fueled this record to the top of the charts. Even when listeners couldn't hear the lyrics, as Vig has noted, they knew that Cobain felt strongly about *something*. You didn't have to understand the

history of rock 'n' roll to understand his anger, sadness, transcendence, and fear.

When Novoselic is asked to analyze the reason the album connected with so many listeners, he is quick to cite the quality of the songs Cobain crafted and their simply melodies. "For mainstream impact," he says, "Kurt's knack for melody and that whole sensibility is something that humans really responded to on a big level. And if you listen to *Nevermind*, it's kind of like a candy rock record but it has a lot of edge."

Critic Grant Alden looks at the record as a milestone in its honesty. "With *Nevermind*, Nirvana pulled off what is the hardest thing for a punk rock band to do: they made an absolutely honest-sounding record that was also in its way commercial," he says. "I don't know if that was what they intended to do, but they did it. I think it's a collection of accidents that this happened. But they managed to be *the* most important band in the world and to be the most *important* band in the world. They earned it. It wasn't a manufactured thing."

For Beehive's Jamie Brown, who had seen the band play live dozens of times before he set up Nirvana's in-store promotion in September

1991, the reason for that importance was emotion: "I think it's one of the most important rock 'n' roll records ever done," he says. "I think important rock 'n' roll records are measured by how they impact people, and the only way that Nirvana impacted people was 100 percent emotional. When you can take teenagers and make them *live* for a rock band, there's got to be something about that. If it wasn't the most important rock record, there hasn't been anything since that was close."

Kim Thayil also suggests that the success of Nirvana reflects larger demographic trends in the population. "I don't think that the record-buying audience switched over from Warrant or Poison to Nirvana or Soundgarden," he asserts. "I just think that a new group of record buyers were coming of age, and the established record buyers were no longer buying albums. The baby-boom generation could only last so long. I think these music executives were being a little arrogant. You do see baby boomers refer to themselves by saying 'We know rock 'n' roll. We grew up with rock 'n' roll. Rock 'n' roll typifies our generation.' Well, it also typifies both generations that were younger and some that were older. Music helps explain to kids how they fit into the world. Sometimes music is a pheromone—they send music out there through the sunroof of their car

At a Dutch radio station.
(Photograph by M. Linssen/Redferns)

and attract like-minded people. It's a little flag or banner. A little scent sent out there.

"The audience for Nirvana was being overlooked by the record companies," Thayil continues. "Those people at Beehive, at the in-store, were a different generation. They grew up with computers and CDs instead of vinyl, and they played videogames in their homes. *Nevermind* was the record to break down those doors and to welcome that generation home."

If Kurt Cobain were around to comment, there's little doubt he would have let the album speak for itself. "Nevermind," he would say, letting his perfect album title be a perfect summation of its own theme and power.

DIVE

It was now one minute before eight on the evening of September 16, 1991, and Kurt Cobain was still in the Beehive record store in Seattle's University District. Fifteen minutes earlier, he and the band had finished their searing set, and now they were back to the normal duties handled at record-store promotions: they were preparing to meet the public. Hundreds of kids had lined up waiting for an autograph, most of them holding CDs to be signed. Some who couldn't afford the new release were holding scraps of paper or portions of the *Nevermind* posters that the crowd had torn off the walls when the band's performance had ended. Some had nothing to get signed; they simply wanted to look into the eyes of the band members and share a moment with their heroes. Many careers in the music business—particularly in the country music field— are built on this sort of glad-handing. Once fans have eyeball contact with a performer, they often feel a personal stake in his or her career and turn into lifelong supporters.

But Nirvana didn't play by those rules, and this event turned out to be one of only a handful of in-stores the band would ever do. Though Cobain was almost universally friendly with the band's fans until the end of 1991 (and Novoselic and Grohl were never anything less than cordial), he never felt comfortable playing the role of rock star or teen idol. Though he certainly never consciously planned it, he made fans for his music the old-fashioned way—by making his songs as personal and as intimate as he dared. The effect was that even kids who had never met Cobain, who had never seen Nirvana play live, who had never been to Aberdeen, who had never had a scrap of napkin signed by Kurt—even kids who could

141

not understand what he was singing because English wasn't their first language—all of these fans and more felt like they knew him personally. And in a way, they *did,* because *Nevermind,* like all great rock 'n' roll albums, transcended the individual story of its authors and became the album of a generation. Anyone who ever listened to this album, from its cocky grandiose beginning of "Here we are now, entertain us . . . ," through its retreat into a dark, murky song about living under a bridge, anyone who even heard "Smells Like Teen Spirit" in passing on the radio, knew the real Kurt Cobain. There was no line between who he was and what his music was, no artifice, no posing, no false front. As Krist Novoselic—who knew Cobain as well as anyone—describes it, "Wherever Kurt came from, he touched something. He was really plugged in to something, and a lot of it was heart. His heart was his receiver, but it was also his transmitter. He would tune in to this stuff and then he would transmit it out."

So it was really no surprise to those who knew Cobain best that after playing the Beehive in-store concert, during the moment in which you'd think most bands would be basking in the glory and excitement of the release of their first major-label album, Kurt did not just sit down and start signing albums for the kids. It's hard to imagine that anything other than the release of *Nevermind* could have been on his mind that day, but Cobain actually had a hidden agenda for agreeing to do this in-store.

Beehive's Jamie Brown says he was surprised when the band agreed to do the in-store in the first place because it was exactly the kind of promotional activity that a major label would pressure a young band to do. Brown was also surprised when the band agreed to actually play at the event, rather than just sign autographs. Even when the band decided to perform, Brown says the initial agreement was that the group would play just a few songs, at most fifteen minutes' worth. He was as shocked as anyone there when the band turned the event into a full-blown concert. "If it wasn't Beehive, which was a cool, noncorporate store, I doubt they would have done it," he says.

After the performance, Brown remembers asking Kurt what he thought of *Nevermind:* "He told me he thought it was good, but he didn't say it in a real overwhelming, confident way. I'd expected him to be the kind of person who would say that his record 'sucked,' and that he wasn't happy with it. But instead, he was pretty happy with it. I remember saying, 'I hope you know how huge this is going to be.' And he looked at

From Beehive through to stadium tours, Cobain always put on a tremendous show.
(PHOTOGRAPH BY NIELS VAN IPEREN/RETNA)

me and kind of nodded his head. Not to say 'Yes,' but to say, 'I'm starting to get the feeling.' It was pretty obvious he wasn't comfortable with what was happening, even by that point. The buzz had already gotten to Kurt and to Nirvana by then."

But Cobain had something to discuss with Brown that, to the singer, was far more important than his upcoming major-label album debut. His "hidden agenda" was probably why he agreed to do the in-store in the first place, because he was not often known to do what his record label asked of him. On Kurt's mind were five copies of a fanzine that he'd brought up with him from Olympia that he wanted the store to carry. "I think it was called either 'Girl Power,' or 'Bicycle Seat,' or 'Bikes without Seats,' something like that," remembers Kelly Canary. "It was a girl one, I'm pretty sure, and it was right around the time of the riot grrl stuff. I think Tobi Vail and Kathleen Hanna wrote for it."

Kurt had stowed the fanzines inside his guitar case. But even though Beehive was a noncorporate store that carried numerous fanzines, their policy was to carry all such publications on consignment only; the fanzine publishers could check in and get paid only if the issues sold. Kurt Cobain—preparing to go on a worldwide three-month tour in two days to promote *Nevermind*—wasn't exactly sure when he'd be coming back to Beehive to collect the money if the fanzines sold. "Here was Kurt," says his label rep, DGC's Susie Tennant, "after this incredible performance, after what some people say was the turning point in [Nirvana's] entire career, and here was Kurt insisting that the store take his friend's fanzine. And at first, the person behind the counter didn't want to do it. They said, 'We can't take them unless it's on consignment.' I was like, 'Dude, just take them! I'll have the label buy them, whatever.'"

"Kurt was more concerned about these fanzines than anything else," remembers Beehive's Brown. "It was his way of appreciating our store, I think, in saying that he wanted these things in there. A friend of his was putting out this fanzine. It wasn't dedicated to one band, but to a lot of bands. There were a lot of cartoons. Actually, I don't even think it was music oriented—it was mostly cartoons. He asked me if we would carry it. Finally, I felt obliged, so I just bought them, so he could get his money and give it to his buddy."

While Novoselic and Grohl began to sign autographs and to greet the gathered masses, the lead singer of Nirvana spent about ten minutes discussing whether the store could carry five copies of a fanzine that sold for two dollars. "To me that was so awesome," says Susie Tennant. "The in-store had been this big thing, and people were going crazy, and everyone was telling Kurt how huge his album was going to be. But when it was all done and over, Kurt just wanted to have these fanzines out there for the kids. That's what it was all about. It wasn't about all the other stuff for him. That's what I remember about Kurt, because that was what was *real*."

Kurt Cobain left the in-store record release for *Nevermind*—an album that in the next year would sell almost ten million copies worldwide—with a ten-dollar bill in his pocket.

SELECTED OFFICIAL
NIRVANA DISCOGRAPHY

Bleach

- LP, U.S., Sub Pop, SP 34.

Nirvana's debut album was originally issued on vinyl LP by Sub Pop in June 1989. The first 1,000 copies were manufactured on solid white vinyl and included a free promotional poster (which showed more of Jason Everman than the rest of the band); the second pressing of 2,000 was on black wax but still came with the poster. Subsequent pressings by Sub Pop were on a variety of different vinyl colors, depending on what pressing plant Sub Pop could obtain credit from. (The label was notorious for switching suppliers whenever their bill ran up too high, which is part of the reason there are many different colored vinyl copies of *Bleach*.) The LP was simultaneously released in Australia by Waterfront Records (DAMP 114) on either blue or yellow wax, with the cover type also in blue or yellow ink. Both the U.S. and Australian first pressings contained the same line-up of songs: Blew/Floyd the Barber/About a Girl/School/Big Cheese/Paper Cuts/Negative Creep/Scoff/Swap Meet/Mr. Moustache/ Sifting.

- LP, U.K., Tupelo, TUP LP6.

On August 12, 1989, Tupelo put out the first U.K. pressing of *Bleach,* with a slightly different track listing (substituting "Love Buzz" for "Big Cheese"). The initial 300 LPs were on white vinyl, while the second 2,000 copies were on green.

- Cassette, U.S., Sub Pop, SP 34a
- CD, U.S., Sub Pop, SP 34b

Also in August 1989, Sub Pop issued the first cassette and CD versions of *Bleach*. The cassette had the same line-up as the initial U.K. release (which added "Love Buzz" to the U.S. line-up) but it also included "Big Cheese" at the end of the tape. The CD release added one more song— "Downer"—tacked on to the end. Tupelo also issued *Bleach* on CD (TUP CD6) and cassette (TUP MC6) in the U.K. around the same time. In April of 1992 *Bleach* was remastered, and rereleased on CD, cassette, and vinyl LP. This new CD version, as issued by Sub Pop, says "digitally remastered" on the CD label and includes the full thirteen songs. In some foreign markets, like the U.K., the CD reissue came out on Geffen as GEF 24433.

Nevermind

- CD, U.S., DGCD 24425
- LP, U.S., DGCC 24425
- Cassette, U.S., DGC 24425

Geffen's DGC imprint simultaneously released *Nevermind* on compact disc, cassette, and vinyl LP on the official release date of September 24, 1991 (copies were sold in many stores several days earlier). The first pressings did not contain "Endless, Nameless" and clocked in at a total time of 42:36. Subsequent pressings of the cassette and CD added this extra track, and the disc has a total time of 59:23. Other than checking the timing or listening to the CD or cassette, there is 8u9 567 no other distinguishing characteristic between the first and second pressings.

- CD, U.S., MFSL UDCD 666
- LP, U.S., MFSL 258

In March 1996, Mobile Fidelity Sound Labs issued audiophile pressings of *Nevermind* both on high-quality virgin vinyl and on a 24-karat gold-plated CD. The pressings both include "Endless, Nameless" and they sound fabulous. A 1996 review in *The Rocket* read: "This CD blows even the vinyl album away. There is more warmth to Kurt's voice, more separation around Krist's bass, and less muddiness around Dave's drums." The audiophile vinyl LP quickly sold out of a limited run and is now out of print as Mobile Fidelity closed their vinyl pressing plant. As of early 1998, the audiophile CD was still in print and it is by far the best way to listen to *Nevermind*.

Incesticide

- CD, U.S., DGC, DGCD 24504
- LP, U.S., DGC, DGC 24504
- Cassette, U.S., DGC, DGCC 24504

On December 15, 1992, Geffen/DGC released *Incesticide* on CD, cassette, and LP. The album was a collection of B-sides, unreleased outtakes, and rarities from the Nirvana vaults—a sticker on the CD billed it as "Rare B-Sides, BBC Sessions, Original Demo Recordings, Outtakes, Stuff Never Before Available." Track listing: Dive/Silver/Stain/Been a Son/Turnaround/Molly's Lips/Son of a Gun/(New Wave) Polly/Beeswax/Downer/Mexican Seafood/Hairspray Queen/Aero Zeppelin/Big Long Now/Aneurysm. The same line-up of songs was featured on all Geffen/DGC releases in countries outside the U.S. The U.S. LP was pressed on blue swirled vinyl and did not include the liner notes by Cobain that were in the CD booklet. The only significant difference in overseas pressings was from Germany, where the promo CD came in a cardboard box that contained three postcards. Though this album was rushed out to take advantage of the phenomenon of Nirvana's 1992 success, it is one of the band's most overlooked records and contains some extraordinary performances. It also contains the work of four Nirvana drummers: Dale Crover, Chad Channing, Dan Peters, and Dave Grohl.

In Utero

- CD, U.S., DGC, DGCD 24536
- LP, U.S., DGC, DGC 24536
- Cassette, U.S., DGC, DGCC 24536

Released in September 1993, this was Nirvana's true follow-up to *Nevermind*. Track listing: Serve the Servants/Scentless Apprentice/Heart-Shaped Box/Rape Me/Frances Farmer Will Have Her Revenge on Seattle/Dumb/Very Ape/Milk It/Pennyroyal Tea/Radio Friendly Unit Shifter/tourette's/All Apologies. In the U.S. the vinyl album was available one week before the CD (vinyl on September 14, 1993; CD on September 21, 1993), though outside the U.S. all formats were released on

September 13, 1993. The limited edition vinyl pressing (15,000 copies) came in several different wax colors including a version that was transparent. Though the U.S. release was otherwise straightforward, in the U.K. and Australia (GEF 24536) the band again included an extra track on the cassette, LP, and CD. In this version the album ended with a song titled "Gallons of Rubbing Alcohol Flow Through the Strip" and clocked in at a total length of 69:05 (the U.S. release times out at 41:20). The extra song is billed as a "Devalued American Dollar Purchase Incentive Track." This song was one of the few tunes in the Nirvana catalog that the band never played live.

- CD, U.S., MFSL UDCD 690

In January 1997, one year after their successful audiophile pressing of *Nevermind,* Mobile Fidelity Sound Labs did the same magic with *In Utero,* releasing it on a 24-karat gold-plated CD. No vinyl version was pressed for this release. This version only includes the standard twelve songs of the regular U.S. pressing. The CD does sound fabulous, and was still in print as of early 1998.

MTV Unplugged in New York

- CD, U.S., DGC, DGCD 24727
- LP, U.S., DGC, DGC 24727
- Cassette, U.S., DGC, DGCC 24727

Released six months after the suicide of Kurt Cobain, *MTV Unplugged in New York* was one of the fastest selling Nirvana albums upon release. The official release date was October 31, 1994, though again vinyl LPs were issued in the U.S. one week early (and again some vinyl editions featured different wax colors including one that was white). The album was simultaneously released worldwide, and no extra tracks were evident in any pressing. (The album did, however, include two songs that weren't part of the original MTV "Unplugged" broadcast.) Track listing: About a Girl/Come As You Are/Jesus Doesn't Want Me for a Sunbeam/The Man Who Sold the World/Pennyroyal Tea/Dumb/Polly/On a Plain/Something in the Way/Plateau/Oh Me/Lake of Fire/All Apologies/Where Did You Sleep Last Night. The session had been recorded for the "Unplugged" television show at Sony Studios, New York on November 18, 1993.

From the Muddy Banks of the Wishkah

- CD, U.S., DGC, DGCD 25105
- LP, U.S., DGC, DGC 25105
- Cassette, U.S., DGC, DGCC 25105

Nirvana's first and only official live album, *From the Muddy Banks of the Wishkah* was released worldwide on October 8, 1996. It had been compiled by Krist Novoselic and Dave Grohl and contains sixteen live tracks from a variety of concerts, stretching from 1989 through 1994. The limited-edition vinyl version came in a two-LP set. Track listing: Intro/School /Drain You/Aneurysm/Smells Like Teen Spirit/Been a Son/Lithium/ Sliver/ Spank Thru/Scentless Apprentice/Heart-Shaped Box/Milk It/ Negatve Creep/Polly/Breed/tourette's/Blew.

"Love Buzz"/"Big Cheese"

- 45, U.S., Sub Pop, SP 23

Nirvana's debut single was released in October of 1988 as the first offering in Sub Pop's Singles Club. "Love Buzz" was a cover of a Shocking Blue song, written by Robby Van Leeuwen, while "Big Cheese" was a Cobain original. Only 1,000 copies were pressed on black vinyl, and each was individually hand-numbered.

Sub Pop 200

- Box set, U.S., Sub Pop, SP 25

This December 1988 release helped put Sub Pop—and Nirvana—on the map. Nirvana's one cut on the three-EP box was "Spank Thru," from the Reciprocal recordings. Other bands included Tad, The Fluid, Mudhoney, Soundgarden, plus others. Only 5,000 copies were made of the box set though both Sub Pop and Tupelo (in the U.K.) rereleased the set on CD in 1990.

Teriyaki Asthma

- 7-inch EP, U.S., C/Z, C/Z 009

Nirvana licensed "Mexican Seafood" to Sub Pop's crosstown Seattle rivals at C/Z Records and it appeared on one of their *Teriyaki Asthma* collections, released in August 1989. The 7-inch also featured tracks by Babes in Toyland and L7 and was limited to 1,000 copies. It was later included on a *Teriyaki Asthma* compilation released in January 1992.

"Blew" EP

- 12-inch EP, U.K., Tupelo, TUP EP 8

This four-song EP was released in December 1989, and though it was originally issued in the U.K., it was commonly distributed in the U.S. also. Track listing: Blew/Love Buzz/Been a Son/Stain.

Hard to Believe: A KISS Covers Album

- CD, U.S., C/Z, CZ 024

Nirvana agreed to contribute a cover of KISS's "Do You Love Me?" for this collection of KISS songs released in August 1990. Other bands on the collection included the Melvins, Skinyard, and Coffin Break. The collection also came out as an LP on C/Z in the U.S., on Waterfront in Australia, and on Southern in the U.K., all in 1990.

"Sliver"/"Dive"

- 45, U.S., Sub Pop, SP 73
- 45, U.K., Tupelo, TUP 25
- 12-inch EP, U.K., Tupelo, TUP EP 25
- CD, U.K., Tupelo, TUP CD 25

Sub Pop's second Nirvana 45 was released in September 1990 and was one of the label's biggest selling singles. The pressing of 3,000 copies was on either blue or pink vinyl; later U.S. pressings were on black wax. The ending of "Sliver" includes an answering machine recording of a conversation between Sub Pop's Jonathan Poneman and Krist Novoselic (who has just been awakened). The 45 was also pressed by Tupelo in the U.K. in January 1991, with a gatefold sleeve, and the first pressing of 2,000 copies was on green vinyl. In April 1991, Tupelo followed up the 45 with a 12-inch EP edition that added a live version of "About a Girl" to the other two songs (delayed because of pressing plant problems). In January 1991, Tupelo also issued a four-track CD rounding out the EP with a live cut of "Spank Thru." (The CD release, strangely, does not include any credits or the name of the label.) The version of "Dive" used on all these releases was the one from Butch Vig's Smart Studios sessions.

"Candy"/"Molly's Lips"

- 45, U.S., Sub Pop, SP 97

In January 1991, Sub Pop released a split single featuring The Fluid's "Candy" backed with Nirvana's "Molly's Lips," a live cover of a Vaselines song. This single was also offered as part of the Sub Pop Singles Club, though some copies were also sold separately. The first pressing of 4,000 copies were printed on green vinyl, while the next pressing of 3,500 featured black vinyl.

"Here She Comes Now"/"Venus in Furs"

- 45, U.S., Communion Records, Communion 23

Nirvana's second split single in June 1991 paired them with their long-time friends the Melvins, who covered "Venus in Furs." Nirvana's contribution was "Here She Comes Now," a Velvet Underground cover, recorded at the Smart Studios sessions. The song also appeared on the Communion album *Heaven and Hell: A Tribute to the Velvet Underground Vol. 1* (released by Imaginary Records in the U.K.).

Backstage pass.

The Grunge Years

- CD, U.S., Sub Pop, SP 112b

Sub Pop released this collection in June 1991, and it included Nirvana's "Dive" from the Smart Studios session.

"Smells Like Teen Spirit"/"Even in His Youth"/"Aneurysm"

- CD5, U.S., DGC, DGCDS 21673

Released on September 10, 1991, this three-song CD was the first dose of the upcoming *Nevermind* and represented Nirvana's first major label release. Geffen not only released this on CD, but also put out a 12-inch vinyl version, a 12-inch picture disc, and even a cassette single (which paired "Smells Like Teen Spirit" with "Drain You"). The CD5 was also released in the U.K. on September 9, 1991 (DCGTD 5), where vinyl and cassette singles also paired "Smells

Like Teen Spirit" with "Drain You." There was a U.S. vinyl single, along with a promotional CD (DGC PRO-CD-4308) that included an edited and unedited version of "Smells Like Teen Spirit."

"On a Plain"

- CD single, U.S., DGC, DGC PRO 4354

In November 1991, DGC released a CD promo of "On a Plain," which led to speculation that the song would be the next single off of *Nevermind.* Cobain had liked the song and early on it had been suggested as one of the potential singles off the record. But when radio stations continued to play "Smells Like Teen Spirit," even several months after its initial release, no other single was forthcoming in 1991.

Hormoaning

- CD, Australia, Geffen, GEFD 21711
- 12-inch EP, Australia, Geffen, GEF 21711
- Cassette, Australia, Geffen, GEFC 21711
- CD, Japan, DGC, MVCG 17002

This 1992 EP from Australia and Japan is one of the most significant rarities in the Nirvana catalog. Track listing: Turnaround/Aneurysm/D-7/Son of a Gun/Even in His Youth/Molly's Lips. This nearly twenty-minute EP was rushed out to take advantage of the band's January 1992 tour of Japan and Australia. The cover has been made to look like an extension of *Nevermind,* with the same typeface and pool background. In Australia, only 5,000 copies were pressed of each format (the 12-inch came on swirled vinyl), and they quickly sold out. The Japanese CD quickly sold out also after the label realized that "D-7" was an uncredited cover of a Wipers song. The eventual release of *Incesticide* included four of these tracks but not "D-7" or "Even in His Youth."

"Come As You Are"/"School"/"Drain You"

- CD5, U.S., DGC, DGCDS 21703

The second single from *Nevermind* could only come out after stations had stopped playing "Smells Like Teen Spirit" so Geffen waited until March 3, 1992, to release "Come As You Are." Both "School" and "Drain You" were live tracks taken from an October 31, 1991, Seattle show at the Paramount. In the U.S. this was released as a CD5, a 12-inch promo, a cassette single, and a CD promo. The CD5 was also released in the U.K. with the same line-up, along with another version that featured "Endless, Nameless" instead of "Drain You." Both vinyl and cassette singles in the U.K. paired "Come As You Are" with "Endless, Nameless" (DGCTD 7).

Eight Songs for Greg Sage and the Wipers

- Box set, U.S., Tim/Kerr Records, TK91EP10 TRIB2

This 1992 release on the Portland-based indie label Tim/Kerr paid homage to one of Cobain's heroes, Greg Sage. Nirvana contributed "Return of the Rat," a cover of a Wipers tune. The set was originally released as four 7-inch singles in a box, but then was reissued in 1993 with the different title of *Fourteen Songs for Greg Sage and the Wipers* with additional tracks.

Nevermind, It's an Interview

- CD promo, U.S., DGC, PRO 4382

In April 1992, Geffen released a promotional CD that contained several live tracks mixed with lengthy interviews with the band conducted by Kurt St. Thomas of Boston radio station WFNX. The interviews were done in early January 1992, and the band gave a detailed accounting of their history, cooperating in a way they rarely did with journalists. Geffen mixed these interviews with a number of live tracks and sent it out to the radio stations, many of which played the CD as a specialty show or cut up the interviews and used the answers to suggest their local DJs were interviewing the band in the studio. Track listing: Breed/Stay Away/School/Mr. Moustache/Sifting/In Bloom/Spank Thru/Floyd the Barber/Scoff/Love Buzz/About a Girl/Dive/Sliver /Aneurysm/Lithium/Even in His Youth/Drain You/Something in the Way/Come As You Are/Polly/In Bloom/Smells Like Teen Spirit/On a Plain/Stay Away/Endless, Nameless/Molly's Lips/Stain/School/Big Cheese/Been a Son/Territorial Pissings/Smells Like Teen Spirit. All the songs were excerpts and incomplete with the exception of "Smells Like Teen Spirit," "Territorial Pissings," "About a Girl," "Drain You," "On a Plain," and "School," the last four being live tracks taken from the October 31, 1991, Seattle concert.

"Lithium"/"Been a Son"/"Curmudgeon"

- CD5, U.S., DGC, DGCDM 21815

The third single from *Nevermind* came out on July 21, 1992, and was snapped up by fans if only because the liner notes contained the complete lyrics to *Nevermind*. "Been a Son" was a live track from the October 31, 1991, Paramount show. The U.S. releases of this track included a promo CD5, a promo 12-inch, a commercial cassette single, and the standard CD5. The CD5 was also released in the U.K., though in a configuration that added "D-7," and in Australia. The U.K. single paired "Lithium" and "Curmudgeon." On the back of the booklet that comes with the U.S. CD5, there is a picture of the Ultrasound image of Frances Bean Cobain, literally "in utero."

"In Bloom"/"Sliver"/"Polly"

- CD5, U.K., DGC, DGCSTP 34

In the U.K. and Australia, a fourth single was broken off from *Nevermind* and issued as a CD5, a 12-inch EP, a picture disc, a vinyl 45, and a cassette single on November 30, 1992. "Polly" was a live version from a Del Mar, California, show of December 28, 1991. In the U.S., there was no "In Bloom" single commercially issued, but, as with "On a Plain," a promotional CD (DGC PRO-CD-4463-2) was sent to radio stations.

"Puss"/"Oh, the Guilt" (The Jesus Lizard/Nirvana split single)

- 45, U.S., Touch and Go, TG83

Nirvana's third split single, released on February 22, 1993, returned them back to the world of indie labels. The Jesus Lizard contributed "Puss" while Nirvana's "Oh, the Guilt" was from an April 1992 Seattle session date, the first post-*Nevermind* session the band had. Though this was an indie record, it came out on 45, cassette, and a CD5 in the U.S.; as a 45, and CD5 in the U.K.; and as a 45 and picture disc in Australia. The U.K. single was on blue vinyl and came with a poster.

No Alternative

- CD, U.S., Arista, 07822 18727 1

Nirvana contributed "Verse Chorus Verse" to this benefit album, which raised money for AIDS research. Because of worry about potential conflict with the forthcoming *In Utero,* Nirvana and their track are not credited on the CD. The CD was also released in the U.K. with the Nirvana track intact.

"Heart-Shaped Box"/"Milk It"/"Marigold"

• CD5, U.K., Geffen, GFSTD 54

On August 23, 1993, Nirvana released their first single from the album that would follow up the tremendous success that was *Nevermind*. But in typical Nirvana fashion, the single wasn't commercially released in the U.S., just in the U.K. and Australia (though many copies were imported into U.S. record stores). In the U.K. it came as a 7-inch, a 12-inch, and a cassette. In the U.S., a promo CD was released, as was a promo 12-inch that paired the song with the only U.S. release of "Gallons of Rubbing Alcohol Flow Through the Strip."

"All Apologies"/"Rape Me"/"Moist Vagina"

• CD5, U.K., Geffen, GFSTD 66

The second single from *In Utero* was also not commercially released in the U.S. though the U.K. issue was imported in droves. The U.K. version listed the B-side as "MV" though in Australia it was titled, correctly, "Moist Vagina." In the U.S., a promotional CD single was released to radio stations but leaving off "Moist Vagina."

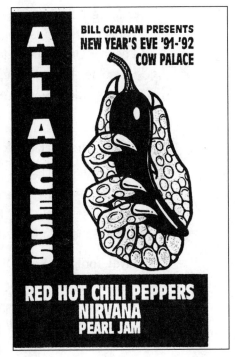

Backstage pass.

The Beavis and Butt-head Experience

• CD, U.S., Geffen, GEFD 24613

This 1993 compilation included Nirvana's "I Hate Myself and Want to Die," an outtake from *In Utero*. The song title had also been seriously considered as a name for the album that was to follow *Nevermind*.

Geffen Rarities Vol. 1

• CD, U.S., DGC, DGCD24553

This 1994 collection included Nirvana's "Pay to Play," taken for the Smart Studios sessions. The CD was also released in Australia.

Home Alive: The Art of Self Defense

• CD, U.S., Epic, E2K 67486

This two-CD collection was released on February 20, 1996, and included tracks donated by forty-seven different artists, mostly from the Northwest. The CD was a benefit for Home Alive, a collective that conducts self-defense training and was formed in honor of murdered Gits singer Mia Zapata. The remaining members of Nirvana agreed to donate "Radio Friendly Unit Shifter" for the CD which was recorded live at a show in Grenoble, France. The compilation also includes songs by Pearl Jam, Soundgarden, Seven Year Bitch, and many other bands.

Videos

1991: The Year Punk Broke

- Video, U.S., DGC, GEV 39518

This 1992 home video release is a documentary of Sonic Youth and Nirvana's tour of Europe in 1991. Track listing: Negative Creep/School/Endless, Nameless/Smells Like Teen Spirit/Polly.

Live! Tonight! Sold Out!!

- Video, U.S., DGC, GEV 39451

This November 1994 home video release was directed by Kevin Kerslake and included interviews and home video footage of the band. Track listing: Aneurysm/About a Girl/Dive/Love Buzz/Breed/Smells Like Teen Spirit/Negative Creep/Come As You Are/Territorial Pissings/Something in the Way/Lithium/Drain You/Polly/Sliver/On a Plain.

Awards

RECORDING INDUSTRY ASSOCIATION OF AMERICA (RIAA) CERTIFICATION (Through January 1, 1998)

Nevermind (LP)	Gold	11/27/91
	Platinum	11/27/91
	Platinum (2)	01/07/92
	Platinum (3)	02/03/93
	Platinum (4)	06/12/92
	Platinum (5)	11/05/93
	Platinum (6)	10/27/94
	Platinum (7)	02/10/95
	Platinum (8 & 9)	10/25/96
"Smells Like Teen Spirit" (single)	Gold	01/22/92
	Platinum	04/01/92

Gold Record Award = 500,000 copies shipped.
Platinum Record Award = 1,000,000 copies shipped.

PERMISSIONS AND CREDITS

SONG AND ALBUM INDEX

GENERAL INDEX

Nirvana
  and achieving correct
    sound, 29–30, 36, 50,
    68, 70
  audience reaction to live,
    4–6
  and capturing live sound in
    the studio, 36, 66, 98
  connection with Butch Vig,
    43
  contractual disputes with
    Sub Pop, 28, 45–46
  early exposure on Sub Pop
    Singles Club, 20
  early following of, in Pacific
    Northwest, 3
  equipment used on
    Nevermind, 60, 61
  as grunge band, 127–28,
    129
  influence of punk rock on,
    18, 63
  and interviewing, 114–16
  and Madison sessions,
    28–32
  major label interest in,
    50–52
  musicality of, 34, 35–36,
    66, 71, 81, 83, 88–89,
    137
  naming of band, 1
  origin of, 16, 18
  popularity of, 3, 139
  as post-punk band, 2
  and problems with Sub Pop,
    45
  and role in Seattle music
    scene, 7, 45, 127
  and search for a drummer,
    18, 20, 43, 47
  and signing with Sub Pop,
    21
  and signing with DGC, 52
  tensions within the band,
    43, 45–46

  and unpreparedness in the
    studio, 29–30, 64
  and writing songs in the stu-
    dio, 28, 64, 90–91
Novoselic, Krist, 2, 5, 8, 23, 56
  as bassist, 36, 38
  and Channing's departure,
    44
  charm of, 29, 61
  on Cobain as songwriter,
    64, 138
  on departing Sub
    Pop, 45
  on "Drain You," 82
  early musical influences
    on, 16
  equipment on Never-
    mind, 62
  on "Here She Comes
    Now," 38
  on "In Bloom," 71
  on Killdozer, 27
  on "Lithium," 39
  and meeting Kurt Cobain,
    16–17
  on mixing of Never-
    mind, 96
  as "musical anchor" of
    Nirvana, 38
  and musical interplay with
    Cobain, 38, 64
  and name change,
    2
  on recording at Smart
    Studios, 27
  sense of humor of, 80, 90,
    108–9, 126
  on "Smells Like Teen Spirit,"
    66, 68, 95
  on "Something in the Way,"
    87, 88
  on songwriting, 10
  on Sound City, 59
  on Butch Vig as pro-
    ducer, 54

ABOUT THE AUTHORS

Jim Berkenstadt is an attorney and journalist based in Madison, Wisconsin. He has written for *Musician, Goldmine, VOX, ICE, Good Day Sunshine*, among other magazines. He is co-author of *Black Market Beatles: The Story Behind the Lost Recordings.*

Charles R. Cross has been editor of *The Rocket* since 1987. He's written for *Rolling Stone, Esquire, Request*, and many other magazines. He is author of *Backstreets, Springsteen: The Man and His Music* and co-author of *Led Zeppelin: Heaven and Hell.*